WITHDRAWN

MAIMONIDES' INTRODUCTION TO HIS COMMENTARY ON THE MISHNAH

MAIMONIDES' INTRODUCTION TO HIS COMMENTARY ON THE MISHNAH

Translated and Annotated
by Fred Rosner

JASON ARONSON, INC.
Northvale, New Jersey
London

This book was set in 13 point Schneidler by TechType of Upper Saddle River, New Jersey, and printed by Haddon Craftsmen in Scranton, Pennsylvania.

Library of Congress Cataloging-in-Publication Data

Maimonides, Moses, 1135–1204.
   [Sirāj. English. Selections]
   Maimonides' Introduction to his commentary on the Mishnah / translated by Fred Rosner.
     p. cm.
   Includes bibliographical references.
   ISBN 1-56821-241-0
   1. Mishnah–Introductions. I. Rosner, Fred. II. Title.
BM497.7.M332513 1995
296.1'2307–dc20   94-14644

Manufactured in the United States of America. Jason Aronson Inc. offers books and cassettes. For information and catalog write to Jason Aronson Inc., 230 Livingston Street, Northvale, New Jersey 07647.

This book is dedicated to the
memory of my father-in-law
RABBI MITCHEL S. ESKOLSKY Z'TL
a tower of spiritual strength, whose face shone
resplendent with the light of Torah

and to the memory of my mother-in-law
MRS. MILDRED ESKOLSKY Z'L
whose devotion to her children and dedication to the
Torah reigned supreme throughout her life.

Contents

Foreword

Aaron D. Twerski

or over two decades I have had the inesti-
mable pleasure of watching at close range
the productivity of Dr. Fred Rosner in
bringing the works of the Rambam to the
English-speaking public. I never cease
to marvel at how he finds the time to practice medicine
at the highest level of professionalism and yet work in
the vineyards of Torah. The only explanation can be
that his love of Torah and his understanding that with
this work he binds himself to the ages sustains him
through this arduous task.

As to the work at hand, I can only say that Dr.
Rosner's translation of this most important work of
the Rambam is clear and lucid. One can sit down at a
single reading and understand the fundamental principles of the *mesorah* of Torah. He has made it marvel-
ously readable.

Every word of the text is holy. Each word gives testament to the unshakable faith of the Rambam in the words of the masters of the Talmud. In dealing with the allegorical passages of the Talmud he states, "If a person encounters one of their sayings which seems to contradict common sense according to his understanding, he should not consider the failure to understand these matters as a defect of the matter themselves; rather one should attribute the failure to inadequacy of one's intellect. . . ." One of the greatest intellects in Jewish history cites the passage in Erubin in which the Talmud relates that "the hearts of the ancients are like the door of an *ulam* but those of the latter generations are not even like the eye of a fine needle."

To those who wish to enter the portals of Torah study, these words need be forever before one's eyes. They are not merely words of humility, they are the truth of Torah. Dr. Rosner brings to this work not only his personal humility but also his deep faith that the words of the ancients are revealed truth. His translation is as honest as he can make it. He has labored to bring the words of the Rambam to us as faithfully as he can.

May the merit of his tireless efforts to disseminate Torah serve as a blessing to Fred, his wife, and his children. May the blessing of *brius hagoof v'hanefesh* be with them for years to come.

Preface

Fred Rosner

oses Maimonides, rabbi, physician, philosopher, and mathematician, was born in Cordova, Spain on March 30, 1138 (*Nisan* 14, 4898). His illustrious ancestry traces back to the royal house of King David of Israel. The task of raising the precocious brilliance of Maimonides' intellect as a child fell upon his father Maimon, his mother having died in childbirth. Constant persecution by the Almohades, a fanatical Arab sect from North Africa, forced the Maimon family to wander throughout Spain, North Africa, and Palestine. They finally settled in Fostat (Old Cairo), Egypt in 1165. During these difficult years, Maimonides wrote a brilliant work on logic (see critical edition by Israel Efros, New York: American Academy for Jewish Research, 1939, pp. 136 [Heb.] and 65 [Eng.], and, at age twenty-three, completed a work on the computation of the Jewish calendar (*Maamar Halbbur*) demonstrating a profound insight into astronomy and mathematics. In 1168, after ten years of effort, his first major work, the *Commentary on the Mishnah* appeared. Ten more years saw the completion of Maimonides' gigantic compilation and codification of biblical and talmudic law in fourteen volumes, the *Mishneh Torah* (translated and published in English in great part by the Yale University Press, 1949–1972). In the year 1190, the third of Maimonides' great works, *The Guide for the Perplexed* (see critical edition by Shlomo Pines, University of Chicago Press, 1963, pp. 658), established beyond doubt his philosophical genius.

Other writings of Maimonides include the *Book of Commandments* (see edition by Charles Chavel, London: Soncino Press, 1967). Commentaries on certain tractates of the Gemara or Talmud (for example Pinchas Shulman's edition of Maimonides' *Commentary on Tractate Rosh Hashanah*, 1958, pp. 216), the *Treatise on Resurrection* (see critical edition by Joshua Finkel, New York: American Academy for Jewish Research, 1939, pp. 42 [Heb.] and 105 [Eng.]), the *Epistle to Yemen* (see critical edition by Abraham Halkin with English translation by Boaz Cohen, New York: American Academy for Jewish Research, 1952, pp. xx, xxxvi, and 109), numerous Responsa (see Joshua Blau's three-volume edition of Maimonides' *Responsa*, Jerusalem: Mekitze Nirdamim, 1958) and ten medical treatises (see *The Medical Writings of Moses Maimonides* by F. Rosner in the *New*

York State Journal of Medicine, September 1973, Vol. 73, pp. 2185–2190).

Although Chief Rabbi of the large Jewish community in Cairo, Maimonides turned to medicine as a livelihood after the tragic death of his brother David and the loss of the family fortune in a shipwreck. Maimonides' fame as a physician spread rapidly, and he was appointed physician to the Royal Court of Saladin, Sultan of Egypt. It is related that during the third Christian Crusade in neighboring Palestine, Richard the Lion-Hearted, King of England, asked Maimonides to become his personal physician, an offer that Maimonides declined.

The many facets of Maimonides as physician, theologian, scientist, philosopher, and writer put a tremendous strain on him as described in the classic letter he wrote to his friend, disciple and most famous of all translators Rabbi Samuel Ibn Tibbon in 1199:

> I live in Fostat and the Sultan resides in Cairo; these two places are two Sabbath limits [marked off areas around a town within which it is permitted to move on the Sabbath; approximately one and a half miles] distant from each other. My duties to the Sultan are very heavy. I am obliged to visit him every day, early in the morning, and when he, any of his children or any one of his concubines are indisposed, I cannot leave Cairo but must stay during most of the day in the palace. It also frequently happens that one or two of the officers fall sick and I must attend to their healing. Hence, as a rule, every day, in the morn-

ing I go to Cairo. Even if nothing unusual happens there, I do not return to Fostat until the afternoon. Then I am famished, but I find the antechambers filled with people, both Jews and Gentiles, nobles and common people, judges and policemen, friends and enemies – a mixed multitude who await the time of my return.

I dismount from my animal, wash my hands, go forth to my patients and entreat them to bear with me while I partake of some light refreshment, the only meal I eat in twenty-four hours. Then I go to attend to my patients and write prescriptions and directions for their ailments. Patients go in and out until nightfall, and sometimes even, as the Torah is my faith, until two hours or more into the night. I converse with them and prescribe for them even while lying down from sheer fatigue. When night falls, I am so exhausted that I can hardly speak.

In consequence of this, no Israelite can converse with or befriend me [on religious or community matters] except on the Sabbath. On that day, the whole congregation, or at least the majority, comes to me after the morning service, when I instruct them as to their proceedings during the whole week. We study a little together until noon, when they depart. Some of them return and read with me following the afternoon service until evening prayers. In this manner, I spend the days. I have here related to you only a part of what you would see if you were to visit me.

Thus, it seems even the more incredible that Maimonides found time to carry on so many pursuits and to indulge in the overwhelming amount of rabbinic, medical, philosophic, and other scientific writings that he did.

Maimonides died on December 13, 1204 (*Tevet* 20, 4965) and was buried in Tiberias, Palestine. The Christian, Moslem, and Jewish worlds mourned him. His literary ability was extraordinary and his knowledge encyclopedic. He mastered nearly everything known in the fields of theology, mathematics, law, philosophy, astronomy, ethics, and medicine. As a rabbi, his leadership was supreme. As a physician, he treated disease by the scientific method and not by rule of thumb. His inspiration lives on through the years and his position as one of the giants of history is indelibly recorded. To the Jewish people he symbolized the highest spiritual and intellectual achievement of man on this earth; as so aptly stated, "From Moses to Moses there never arose a man like Moses," and none has since.

Introduction

Fred Rosner

Description of the Mishnah

The Jewish people believe in the fundamental principle that Moses received the Torah from God on Sinai and transmitted it to the children of Israel. The Pentateuch (or Five Books of Moses) represents the written Torah, whereas the explanations, interpretations, and teachings of the written law are called the Oral Law. The latter was taught by word of mouth from generation to generation and was thus constantly repeated; hence the word *mishnah*, which means to repeat. During times of great stress following the destruction of the Holy Temple, Rabbi Judah the Prince, also known simply as Rebbe, compiled the teachings of the 150 *Tanna'im* (Teachers or Sages) of the time, teachings that were handed down through the centuries from Moses at Sinai, and wrote them down in the second or third century. (The exact date is in dispute.) This work is called the Mishnah. The major architects of this work, in addition to Rabbi Judah the Prince, were Rabbi Hillel, Rabbi Yohanan ben Zakkai, and Rabbi Akiba. The Mishnah is thus not the work of one man or even several men but a composite of centuries of teachings. For this reason it soon attained canonical authority.

The Mishnah consists of six orders or major divisions (Hebrew word for order is *seder*, plural *sedarim*), which in turn are subdivided to produce a total of sixty-one tractates of the Mishnah listed below (63 if Bava Kamma, Bava Metzia, and Bava Batra are considered separately). Each tractate is further subdivided into chapters, of which the total number is 524. The comprehensive commentary on the Mishnah that forms the largest portion of the Oral Law is the Gemara or "Teaching." The word *Gemara* is sometimes used synonymously with the word *Talmud*, although, in the strict sense, both Mishnah and Gemara make up the Talmud. The Gemara explains terms and subjects of the Mishnah, seeks to elucidate difficulties, clarifies discrepancies in the Mishnah, provides lengthy debates and discussions upon which legal decisions of the Mishnah are based, and is the backbone for the proper understanding of the written law or Pentateuch. The Mishnah was written in Hebrew in contradistinction to the Gemara, which is mostly in Aramaic. For a detailed discussion of the purpose, character, origin, development, arrangement, language, text, and editions of the Mishnah, the interested reader is referred to the introduction to Canon Danby's *The Mishnah* (Oxford University Press, 1958, pp. xxxii and 844).

The six orders (Sedarim) and sixty-one tractates of the Mishnah arranged according to Maimonides' *Introduction to Seder Zeraim* are as follows:

I. Seder Zera'im (Seeds)

1. Tractate Berakhot (Benedictions). Deals with prayer, benedictions, and worship.
2. Tractate Pe'ah (Corners). Deals with corners of the field to be left to the poor.
3. Tractate Demai (Doubtful). Deals with produce that may or may not have been tithed.
4. Tractate Kilayim (Mixtures). Deals with prohibitions of mixtures in plants, animals and garments.
5. Tractate Shevi'it (Seventh). Deals with the laws of the Sabbatical year.
6. Tractate Terumot (Heave Offerings). Deals with laws of produce to be given to the Priest.
7. Tractate Maaserot (Tithes). Deals mainly with laws of the first tithe.
8. Tractate Maaser Sheni (Second Tithe). Deals with the laws of the second tithe.
9. Tractate Hallah (Dough). Deals with laws of portions of dough to be given to the Priest.

10. Tractate Orlah (Uncircumcised or foreskin). Deals with the prohibition of the use of trees during the first three years after planting.
11. Tractate Bikkurim (First fruits). Deals with laws of the first fruits.

II. Seder Mo'ed (Festivals)

1. Tractate Shabbat (Sabbath). Deals with laws pertaining to the Sabbath.
2. Tractate Eruvin (Fusions). Deals with laws pertaining to fusing abodes or domains on the Sabbath.
3. Tractate Pesahim (Pascal Lambs). Deals with laws of Passover.
4. Tractate Shekalim (Shekels). Deals with laws pertaining to the payment of the shekel tax for the Temple upkeep.
5. Tractate Yoma (The Day). Deals with laws of the Day of Atonement.
6. Tractate Sukkah (Booth). Deals with laws of the Feast of Tabernacles.
7. Tractate Betzah (Egg). Deals with laws pertaining to festivals in general.
8. Tractate Rosh Hashanah (Head of the Year). Deals with laws pertaining to the New Year.
9. Tractate Taanit (Fasts). Deals with laws pertaining to fast days.
10. Tractate Megillah (Scroll). Deals with laws pertaining to the Book of Esther and Purim.

11. Tractate Mo'ed Katan (Minor Festival). Deals with laws of semifestive times.
12. Tractate Hagigah (Festal Offering). Deals with laws pertaining to the thrice yearly pilgrimage to Jerusalem.

III. Seder Nashim (Women)

1. Tractate Yevamot (Sisters-in-law). Deals with laws of Levirate marriage and prohibited marriages.
2. Tractate Ketubot (Marriage Settlements). Deals with laws pertaining to marriage settlements.
3. Tractate Nedarim (Vows). Deals with laws pertaining to vows.
4. Tractate Nazir (Nazarite). Deals with laws pertaining to Nazarite vows.
5. Tractate Gittin (Divorces). Deals with laws pertaining to divorces.
6. Tractate Sotah (Suspected Adulteress). Deals with laws pertaining to a suspected adulteress.
7. Tractate Kiddushin (Consecration). Deals with laws pertaining to betrothal and marriage.

IV. Seder Nezikin (Damages)

1a. Tractate Bava Kamma (First Gate). Deals with laws pertaining to personal and property damage as well as compensations.

1b. Tractate Bava Metzia (Middle Gate). Deals with laws pertaining to found property.

1c. Tractate Bava Batra (Last Gate). Deals with laws of ownership, acquisition, division, and inheritance of property.

2. Tractate Sanhedrin (Higher Courts). Deals with laws of the composition, powers, and functions of higher courts.

3. Tractate Makkot (Beatings). Deals with laws of judicial floggings.

4. Tractate Shevu'ot (Oaths). Deals with laws pertaining to various types of oaths.

5. Tractate Eduyot (Testimonies). A collection of miscellaneous traditions.

6. Tractate Avodah Zarah (Strange Worship). Deals with rites and cults of idolaters.

7. Tractate Avot (Fathers). Contains aphorisms and maxims of ethics and morality.

8. Tractate Horayot (Rulings). Deals with erroneous rulings of religious courts.

V. Seder Kodashim (Holy Things)

1. Tractate Zevahim (Sacrifices). Deals with laws of animal sacrifices.

2. Tractate Menahot (Meal Offerings). Deals with laws of meal and drink offerings.

3. Tractate Hullin (Non-Holy). Deals with laws of slaughtering for normal consumption. Also contains the dietary laws.

4. Tractate Bekhorot (Firstborn). Deals with laws of the first born of man and animals.
5. Tractate Arakhin (Estimations). Deals with laws pertaining to the ransom of Holy Objects.
6. Tractate Temurah (Substitution). Deals with laws pertaining to substitution of one offering for another.
7. Tractate Keritot (Extirpations). Deals with offenses for which *Karet* (heavenly punishment) is the penalty.
8. Tractate Me'ilah (Trespass). Deals with the laws of sacrilege.
9. Tractate Tamid (Permanent). Deals with the laws pertaining to the "permanent" or daily sacrifices.
10. Tractate Middot (Measures). Deals with measurements of the Temple, its gate, Courts, halls, and altar.
11. Tractate Kinnim (Nests). Deals with laws pertaining to bird offerings.

VI. Seder Tohorot (Purifications)

1. Tractate Keilim (Vessels). Deals with laws pertaining to uncleanness of vessels.
2. Tractate Oholot (Tents). Deals with laws of defilement conveyed by a corpse.
3. Tractate Nega'im (Leprosies). Deals with laws pertaining to leprosy.

4. Tractate Parah (Heifer). Deals with laws pertaining to the red heifer.
5. Tractate Tohorot (Purifications). Deals with laws of defilement of foods and liquids.
6. Tractate Mikva'ot (Ritual Immersion Pools). Deals with laws pertaining to ritual baths and pools.
7. Tractate Niddah (Menstruant). Deals with laws of menstruation.
8. Tractate Makhshirin (Predispositions). Deals with conditions causing predisposition to uncleanness.
9. Tractate Zavim (Sufferers of Flux). Deals with laws pertaining to those with an issue.
10. Tractate Tevul Yom (Immersed at Daytime). Deals with laws pertaining to a man unclean until sundown.
11. Tractate Yadayim (Hands). Deals with laws of uncleanness due to unwashed hands.
12. Tractate Uktzin (Stems). Deals with laws pertaining to defilement of stalks, skin, seeds, and stems of fruits.

Description of Maimonides' Commentary on the Mishnah

The father of all Mishnah commentators is the great French scholar, biblical and rabbinical interpreter, Rabbi Shlomo Yitzhaki, known more popularly simply as Rashi (1040–1105). His Commentary is printed in every edition of the Babylonian Talmud, side by side with the main text.

Moses Maimonides' (1138–1204) Commentary on the Mishnah was the second major commentary on the entire Mishnah and is broader than that of Rashi, and contains lengthy digressions to propound general principles of Judaic law and religious practices and faith.

Other early commentators include Isaac ben Malkhizedek of Siponto, Italy (1110–1170), Samson ben Abraham of Sens, France (1150–1231) and Asher ben Yehiel of Germany (c. 1250–1327).

The two most highly regarded Mishnah commentators today, printed in nearly every edition of the Mishnah, are Rabbi Obadiah ben Abraham of Bertinoro, an Italian Jew of the fifteenth century whose work is based mainly on Rashi, and Rabbi Yom Tov Lippman Heller (1579–1654), popularly known as the Tosefot Yom Tov. The Commentary of the latter is an erudite, critical supplement to the simpler but quite adequate Commentary of the Rabbi of Bertinoro.

The most recent giant of Mishnah commentators was Rabbi Israel Lipschutz (1782–1860). His commentary, known as the Tiferet Israel, is printed in many modern Mishnah texts.

The Name of the Commentary

The *Commentary on the Mishnah* by Moses Maimonides is popularly known as "The Luminary" (*Sefer Hamoar* in Hebrew; *Kiteb El Siraj* in Arabic). Whether Maimonides himself introduced this name or whether he referred to his work simply as *The Commentary on the Mishnah* is unclear. Moritz Steinschneider, the famous Hebrew bibliographer, is of the latter opinion. He states, in his monumental work *Die Hebraische Ubersetzungen des Mittelalters und Die Juden als Dolmetscher*, (Berlin, 1893) that the name "Luminary" was given by later generations and not by Maimonides himself. The first reference to the name "Luminary" is to be found in Rabbi Menachem Ben Zerakh's fourteenth century work *Tseda Laderech* in which he states that Maimonides called his work *Sefer Hamoar* or "Luminary." In either event, the name "Luminary" is very appropriate since the major purpose of Maimonides' work was to shine light upon the stenographic brevity of the Mishnah. In this effort he succeeded brilliantly.

The Introduction to Seder Zera'im

In the introduction to Tractate Berakhot, more popularly known as the *Introduction to Seder Zera'im*, which serves as the general introduction to the entire Commentary, Maimonides reviews the story of Sinai and the teachings of God transmitted through Moses to Aaron, then to the latter's sons, then to the elders, and then to all the children of Israel. Maimonides re-creates the receiving of the Torah by the Israelites at Sinai, and thus provides a beautiful historical account and description of the development of the Oral Law. He points out the harmony between the Oral and Written Laws, and describes Moses as the greatest of all prophets. We thus have, in this introduction, a complete history of Jewish tradition from its Sinaitic origin to the time of the compilations of the Mishnah and the Gemara.

A lengthy description of prophecy is given. According to Maimonides, the subject of prophecy requires very careful consideration. He states that average people are under the misconception that a prophet must perform miracles to prove his divine nobility. This is erroneous. Maimonides further describes types of prophets under two main headings: those who prophesy in the name of idolatry and those who prophesy in the name of the Holy One, Blessed be He. Also related by Maimonides are the manner of testing a prophet as to his authenticity and the manner of punishment to be administered if the prophet is found to be false. Three prerequisites to becoming a prophet are

1. Profound knowledge and understanding of God, of man and the world
2. An ability to control one's passions
3. Complete contentment with one's lot

Maimonides then provides a classification of the various types of laws contained in the Mishnah. All

INTRODUCTION

the laws received by Moses and enunciated in the Mishnah can be classified into five categories:

1. Explanations derived from scriptural allusions and implications through logical means, and concerning which no disagreement exists between Sages
2. Laws given to Moses at Sinai without scriptural proof
3. Laws derived through logical means in which argumentation between Sages occurs and where the final ruling is according to the majority view
4. Decrees ordained by Sages and Prophets in every generation to protect the Torah
5. Laws performed by virtue of their being accepted custom but without scriptural decree

Maimonides then describes the intent of the compiler of the Mishnah, Rebbe, or Rabbi Judah the Prince in subdividing all this information into the following six sections or orders:

1. Seder Zera'im
   Laws dealing with growths from the earth such as the laws of Orlah (prohibition of the use of trees during the first three years after planting), tithes, heave offerings, and other priestly dues
2. Seder Mo'ed
   Laws dealing with the times and festivals of the

year, and what is permitted and what is prohibited during these times
3. Seder Nashim
   Laws pertaining to the relationships between man and woman, including such items as marriage and divorce
4. Seder Nezikin
   Laws pertaining to dealings between men in business ventures of all types
5. Seder Kodashim
   Laws of Sacrifices, the holy Temple, and its contents
6. Seder Tohorot
   Laws of purifications and their opposites

Following this, Maimonides considers every individual tractate of each order of the Mishnah. He remarks that Berachot is the first tractate because it contains the duties of reciting benedictions, which are daily obligations upon us. He then discusses the reasons why each tractate follows or precedes the tractate that it does, and shows an orderly sequence in the consecutive listing of the various tractates and orders. No subject matter is considered out of context or out of sequence from the logical succession of expositions and interpretations of rabbinic and biblical law.

Maimonides then describes the *Tosefta* (supplemental Mishnah) and *Beraita* (extraneous Mishnah), their purpose and their authorship. This is followed by an account of the compilation of the Gemara or Babylonian Talmud by Rav Ashi. The four reasons that-prompted Rav Ashi to redact this work are given by Maimonides as follows:

1. To explain the Mishnah and its contents
2. To provide background for the final ruling in a matter concerning which two Sages differ in opinion
3. To provide new interpretations for legal matters discussed in the Mishnah
4. To provide homiletical expositions and moral teachings

Maimonides then goes into a lengthy side discussion of the value and necessity of homiletical exposition, including a protracted dissertation on knowledge and wisdom and understanding of the existence of living and inanimate things, and the purpose of the world and all that is contained therein.

Following this, Maimonides speaks briefly of the redaction of the Palestinian or Jerusalem Talmud by Rabbi Yohanan. Examples are then given of the post-talmudic Sages, the Geonim, and some of their works of commentary on the Talmud. Maimonides then states that his own Commentary on the Mishnah is derived in great part from the teachings of his revered father, Rabbi Maimon, and from Rabbi Joseph Halevi.

He describes the benefits to be derived from his Commentary:

1. To learn the true meaning of the Mishnah
2. To enunciate final rulings in the Mishnah
3. To serve as an introduction to the study of the Talmud
4. To serve as a permanent record of mishnaic knowledge

The final section of Maimonides' Introduction to the *Commentary on the Mishnah* deals with lineage and genealogy and enumeration of the Sages of the Mishnah. This is accomplished in ten small treatises within the introduction. The first treatise or chapter lists the Sages found in the Mishnah in whose names final rulings were enunciated. The second chapter enumerates the Sages mentioned in the Mishnah because of an occurrence that once happened to them or because of a teaching they once expounded. The third chapter deals with the ancestry of various Sages of the Mishnah. The fourth chapter deals with Sages whose life spans overlay two generations. The fifth chapter enumerates teacher and disciple pairs of Sages. The sixth chapter attempts to clarify the identity of Sages mentioned by first name only. The seventh chapter deals with the seniority of the Sages, and the eighth describes some of their professions, native lands, and families. The ninth chapter lists the Sages who frequently voiced differences of opinion from their colleagues, and the tenth chapter deals with the frequency of occurrence of certain Sages' names throughout the Mishnah.

This concludes the introduction to Seder Zera'im. The introduction, as the rest of the Commentary, is simple, concise, and orderly. Much is said in few words in spite of the lengthy side discussions of very basic tenets in Judaism that Maimonides stresses and expounds upon in various places of this work.

The other introductions to the other orders of the Mishnah are all luminous masterpieces of exposition and interpretation of involved, obscure, and difficult subjects. Some of the more important ones are described in the next section.

General Content of the Commentary

Maimonides' aim in writing his *Commentary on the Mishnah* was to popularize the Mishnah. He penetrated all ramifications of the subject matter contained in the Mishnah: moral, ethical, social, theological, scientific, and philosophical. Maimonides' major literary assets, according to Graetz, are his abilities for clarity, methodology, and symmetry, qualities in great part lacking in the Talmud. The Commentary was written in the Arabic vernacular because this was the language understood by most Jews at the time and, to some, the only language. Thus, Maimonides made the Mishnah accessible to all, layman and scholar alike. He made the

Mishnah easily understood by the logic, simplicity, and brevity of his style. He detached the essential "legal decision" from the mass of talmudic debate upon which it is based and in which it was often obscured. He did a great deal more than just provide a literal interpretation of the Mishnah text. He commented and philosophized on it.

It is all the more remarkable that Maimonides wrote this great work at a time when he labored under great burdens and hardships. He was exiled from country to country; he was a victim of the hatred of his times; he was a true "wandering Jew" without reference material or libraries at his disposal. His mind was a photographic repository of all that he ever learned. He was unyielding in his efforts to complete this work and did so after ten years, completing it in the year 1168 at age thirty.

One of the most famous parts of the Commentary is the introduction to tractate Avot, which represents the unique psychological treatise on the health and sickness of the soul and its reversion to health. This treatise is popularly known as the "Eight Chapters" (see Joseph Gorfinkle's critical edition *The Eight Chapters of Maimonides on Ethics*, New York: Columbia University Press, 1912, pp. 104 [Eng.] and 55 [Heb.]). It is one of the places in the Commentary where Maimonides departs from his brevity and conciseness and makes excursions into lengthy discussions of ethics, morality, theology, and philosophy, or a scientific subject such as astrology, astronomy, or mathematics. In Chapter 4 of the "Eight Chapters," Maimonides propounds the famous Aristotelian doctrine of the mean. He states that excess or deficiency, the two extremes, are both evil. A "middle of the road" path is desirable in Greek virtues such as bravery, temperament, and magnanimity, as well as in Hebraic virtues such as humility and charity.

The combination and synchronism between Greek metaphysics and Hebrew revelation is well personified by the following two quotations from the "Eight Chapters": "Ethics are the medicine of the soul" and "All thine actions shall be to the glory of God," the former being the Greek view and the latter the mishnaic outlook.

Equally famous in the Commentary is the description of the *Thirteen Articles or Principles of the Jewish Faith*, which are enumerated and expounded upon in detail in Chapter 10 of tractate Sanhedrin. This description is combined with a discussion of the world to come. The first Mishnah in Chapter 10 in Tractate Sanhedrin begins with the words "Every Israelite has a share in the world to come." These words are immortalized and recited in most synagogues at the beginning of the Sabbath afternoon recitation of the Ethics of Our Fathers (tractate Avot) during the summer months. To answer the questions as to who is an Israelite and what is the world to come, Maimonides goes into a lengthy explanation of the concepts of immortality. He laments for those who view eternal bliss in the materialistic sense as a Garden of Eden with milk and honey flowing abundantly. His main theme is that man should obtain wisdom for wisdom's sake, obey for obedience's sake, and not be "Like the servants who minister to their master on condition of receiving a reward" (tractate Avot, Chapter 1, Mishnah 3).

Then follows the formulation and description of the thirteen fundamental principles of Judaism. The first five of these deal with the existence of God, that He is the Creator, that He is Incorporeal, Eternal, and alone worthy of man's praise and worship.

Principles six through nine are concerned with prophecy and revelation. Principles ten and eleven are the beliefs in reward and punishment for observance or transgression of God's commandments, and the final two principles deal with salvation and resurrection.

The following in prose form are the thirteen fundamental beliefs of Judaism as enunciated by Maimonides:

1. I believe with perfect faith that the Creator, blessed be His name, is the Creator and Guide of all created beings and that He alone has made, does make, and will make all things.

2. I believe with perfect faith that the Creator, blessed be His name, is One, and that there is no Unity in any form like His, and that He alone is our God who was, is, and will be.

3. I believe with perfect faith that the Creator,

blessed be His name, is not a body, and that no bodily occurrences happen to Him, and that there exists nothing whatever that resembles Him.

4. I believe with perfect faith that the Creator, blessed be His name, is the first and the last.

5. I believe with perfect faith that the Creator, blessed be His name, is the only one to whom it is proper to pray, and that it is not proper to pray to any being besides Him.

6. I believe with perfect faith that all the words of the prophets are true.

7. I believe with perfect faith that the prophecy of Moses, our Teacher, was true, and that he was the father (i.e., chief or head) of all prophets, both of those who preceded him, and of those who followed him.

8. I believe with perfect faith that the entire Torah that we now possess is the same that was given to Moses our Teacher, may he rest in peace.

9. I believe with perfect faith that the Torah will not be changed, and that there will never be another Torah from the Creator, blessed be His name.

10. I believe with perfect faith that the Creator, blessed be His name, knows every action of the children of men, and all their thoughts, as it is said: *He that fashioned the hearts of them all, that considereth all their doings* (Psalm 33:15).

11. I believe with perfect faith that the Creator, blessed be His name, bestows good upon those who

observe His commandments, and punishes those who transgress His commandments.

12. I believe with perfect faith in the coming of the Messiah and, although he may tarry, in spite of this I will wait daily for his coming.

13. I believe with perfect faith that there will be a revival of the dead at the time when it will please the Creator, blessed be His Name, and exalted be His name for ever and ever.

Many poems have been written incorporating these thirteen doctrines. Among the most noted is the *Yigdal* prayer, authored by *Dayan* Daniel ben Judah in Rome, circa 1300. This prayer is recited at the outset of the morning service, daily. The following is the poetic rendition of Maimonides' thirteen fundamental principles of Judaism, the *Yigdal* prayer:

1. May the living God be exalted and praised,
   He exists; His existence has no limit in time.
2. He is one, and there is no unity like unto His unity,
   He is inconceivable, and His unity is unending.
3. He has no semblance of body, He is incorporeal,
   To His holiness we can naught compare.
4. He preceded all that was created,
   He is first, though His existence had no beginning.

5. Behold, He is the Lord of the Universe,
   To each creature He teacheth His greatness and
   His sovereignty.
6. The rich gift of His prophecy He gave
   To the men of His choice and His glory.
7. Never has there arisen in Israel like unto Moses,
   the Prophet who beheld God's image.
8. A law of truth God gave unto His people,
   By the hand of His prophet, faithful in His
   house.
9. God will not alter nor change His law
   Ever for any other.
10. He watcheth and knoweth our secret thoughts,
    He beholdeth the end of a thing at its incep-
    tion.
11. He bestoweth kindness upon man according to
    his deeds,
    He giveth evil to the wicked according to his
    wickedness.
12. He will send our anointed one at the end of the
    days,
    To redeem those who wait for the end—His
    salvation.
13. God will revive the dead with His great
    kindness,
    Blessed be His glorious name for evermore.

These principles were severely attacked, mainly by
people who asserted that it was temerity on the part of

Maimonides to select only thirteen of the many doctrines of Judaism. Others objected on the grounds that
some of the articles are not based on Judaism at all, or
are not indispensable foundations of our religion. Two
of the most famous of Maimonides' critics in this
regard were Rabbi Abraham ben David, and the philosopher Hasdai Crescas. A partial answer to some of
these criticisms was given by Maimonides in his *Treatise on Resurrection* (critical edition by Joshua Finkel, New
York: American Academy for Jewish Research, 1939,
pp. 42 [Heb.] and 105 [Eng.]).

There are many sections of the Mishnah that have
no Gemara to help clarify certain details, or discuss
certain subjects that the Mishnah describes. These are
most beautifully dealt with by Maimonides in Seder
Tohorot. With the exception of tractate Niddah, no
Gemara exists for the entire Seder Tohorot, which
contains twelve tractates dealing with many difficult
subjects requiring mathematical genius and knowledge
of astronomy for proper interpretation. Maimonides
accomplished his task to perfection, since his Introduction and Commentary on the various subdivisions of
Seder Tohorot (Cleanness) show mastery of talmudic
scholarship.

Although it did not meet with immediate universal
approval and recognition among talmudic scholars,
Maimonides' *Commentary on the Mishnah* remains one of
the outstanding works of rabbinic interpretation of the
Oral Law of the Torah.

Only Extant Manuscript in Maimonides' Own Handwriting

There is still some dispute as to the authenticity of an unusual document that many claim to have been written by Maimonides himself. This most unique manuscript has recently been published in massive volumes by Ejnar Munksgaard in Copenhagen under the title *Maimonidis' Commentarius in Mischnam.* Volume One of the work contains photographic facsimiles of Mishnah Orders Zera'im and Mo'ed as well as the famous introduction to Seder Zera'im. Volume Two contains Mishnah Orders Nashim and part of Nezikin. Volume Three contains the second part of Nezikin and Order Kodashim. The document itself was originally written in six parts, of which only five are extant. Of the Order Tohorot, only a single leaf of a draft version of the Commentary remains in the possession of the Jewish Theological Seminary of America in New York. Order Zera'im is now Manuscript #295 of the Edward Pococke Collection at the Bodleian Library. Seder Mo'ed and Seder Nashim form Manuscripts #72 and #73, respectively, of the Sassoon Library at Letchworth, Hertfordshire, England (Sassoon Catalogue "Ohel David," pp. 92–93).

Dr. Solomon D. Sassoon proves at great length that this manuscript is indeed in Maimonides' handwriting using three main lines of evidence:

1. An inscription on the opening page of Seder Zera'im written and signed by the great-grandson of Maimonides, Rabbi Solomon, in which he clearly states that this work is in the handwriting of his illustrious ancestor "our teacher Moses."

2. Analysis of the handwriting shows it to be identical with other known and undisputed samples of Maimonides' handwriting. Dr. Sassoon describes very detailed measurements of letters, linked letters, spacing between words and between letters, superlinear marks, margins, paragraphing, and the like, which seem to leave little doubt as to the authenticity of Maimonides' handscript.

3. Various references from other manuscripts written in the succeeding three or four centuries.

As mentioned above, *Seder Zera'im* is now Manuscript #117 of the Huntington Collection in the Bodleian Library. It is the same manuscript that is numbered #393 in A. Neubauer's *Catalogue of the Hebrew Manuscripts in the Bodleian Library*, Oxford, 1886. Column #1142 in Neubauer's catalogue cites the following opening poem to Manuscript #393:

ספר אשר חובר בדין משה ביאור הלכותיו ודת צדקו

כדת אשר העתיק[1] זקינינו[2] בוניו אשר הם חזקו בדקו[3]

---

1. Sassoon renders this word העתיקו.
2. See Proverbs 25:1.
3. See 2 Kings 12:6–7.

חבור שפל כח צעיר שנים משה בנו מימון אשר צעקו
אל אל ליישר את נתיבותיו לשום בתורתו לבד חשקו
לנפול חבלים לו בחר[4] הבין לאכול פרי חכמה[5] לבד חקו
אז יחזה טוב אל[6] ואז ישמח משה[7] ביופי מתנת חלקו

Sassoon's translation of the opening poem to Manuscript #393 is as follows:

The work which deals with the laws of Moses
[i.e., the Mishnah]
a Commentary on its Rules and Righteous ways
Based upon traditions handed down by our Sages
its builders who strengthened its structure [i.e.,
the *Amora'im*]
Composed by one who is weak and young in
years
Moses the son of Maimon who cried
To God to make his path straight and to put his
desire in his law only
In order that he might win a plot on the Mountain
of Knowledge
and that he might eat only of the fruit of
wisdom as his daily fare
Then he shall see the goodness of God and then
Moses shall
delight in the beauty of his lot.

---

4. Sassoon renders this word בחר. See Psalm 16:6.
5. Probable reference to Genesis 2:9.
6. See Psalm 17:15.
7. From the Sabbath morning service.

My rendition of this poem is as follows:

The work which was composed according to the
     Law of Moses
     the explanation of its regulations and its just
     statute
As the Statute recorded by our Elders, its builders,
     who strengthened its structure,
Was composed by one who is weak and young in
     years,
     Moses the son of Maimon who cried
To God to straighten his paths and to put his
     desire
     only to his Torah,
Who chose understanding to be his estate,
     to eat only from the fruit of wisdom as his daily
     fare
Then shall he see the goodness of God and then
     shall
     Moses rejoice in the beauty of his lot.

Early Translations and Editions

The earliest printed edition of the Mishnah, published
in Naples in 1492 in folio by the Soncino Press,
contains Maimonides' Commentary. A copy of this
entire precious work is in the Jewish Theological

Seminary Library in New York. This edition was followed by the folio edition of Riva di Trento in 1559. Then appeared the quarto edition of Sabbionetta and Mantua in 1559–1563, a copy of which is extant in the Library of Congress in Washington, D.C., as well as the folio edition of Venice in 1606 containing the commentaries of both Maimonides and Bertinoro.

Most modern editions of the Babylonian Talmud contain a Hebrew translation of Maimonides' *Commentary on the Mishnah,* and occasional Mishnah texts are still available with Maimonides' Commentary, also in Hebrew. This standard Hebrew version of Maimonides' Commentary is the work of the following six early translators, dating back to the thirteenth century.

Rabbi Judah ben Shlomo Al Harizi

Harizi began translating the Commentary on Seder Zera'im from Arabic into Hebrew in Marseilles, France, during the lifetime of Maimonides. He completed the task in two years, finishing it in Rome. Only the Introduction and the first five tractates of Zera'im are incorporated into standard editions of the Talmud today, however, the last six tractates of Harizi's translation having been lost. Rabbi Harizi describes three prerequisites for a translator:

1. Mastery of the language from which one is translating
2. Mastery of the language into which one is translating
3. Mastery of the subject matter

Rabbi Joseph ben Isaac ben Al Fawwal

Rabbi Joseph translated Seder Mo'ed in the town of Huesca, Spain. The translation of the last six chapters of Seder Zera'im in modern editions of the Talmud is also attributed to him, as he himself states in his introduction to tractate Terumot: "I searched throughout the land for a copy of Seder Zera'im and found thereof only from the beginning [of Seder Zera'im] to the end of tractate Shevi'it of the copy of the wise, great Sage and most knowledgeable translator, Rabbi Judah Harizi. Of the remaining tractates I found naught." He further states that although his "lot" was to translate Seder Mo'ed, at the beckoning of Rabbi Solomon Adarat, he also undertook to translate the last six tractates of Seder Zera'im. Thus, although Al Harizi did translate the entire Seder Zera'im, the translations of the last six tractates thereof extant today in most copies of the Talmud are those of Al Fawwal.

Rabbi Jacob ben Moses ben Akhsai

Rabbi Jacob, in the province of Aragon, Spain, was assigned the task of translating Seder Nashim, which he did with the able assistance of Rabbi Chaim ben Solomon the physician, ben Beka. This was at the request of Rabbi Simhah, an emissary from the Jewish Sages of Rome.

Rabbi Solomon ben Joseph ben Jacob

Rabbi Solomon in Saragossa, Spain, was assigned the task of translating Seder Nezikin. This was also at the beckoning of the sages of Rome, through their emissary Rabbi Simhah. Rabbi Solomon was a physician and translated all of Seder Nezikin except tractate Avot, which had already been translated by the most illustrious of all Maimonides' translators, Rabbi Samuel Ibn Tibbon.

Rabbi Samuel ben Judah ben Tibbon

Rabbi Samuel was one of a renowned family of translators. At the request of the Sages of Lunel, France, he translated tractate Avot, together with the *Guide for the Perplexed*, which Maimonides had also written in Arabic.

Rabbi Nathaniel the Physician ben Jose ben Almoli

The commission of Rabbi Simhah from the Sages of Rome was completed when he assigned the translations of Seder Kodashim and Seder Tohorot to Rabbi

Nathaniel. The latter accepted the task reluctantly, saying he had only one or two Arabic manuscripts at his disposal and could, therefore, not vouch for the accuracy of the work. Furthermore, he declared, he was a physician and possessed inadequate talmudic scholarship. In spite of these difficulties, he succeeded in the great work he had undertaken.

Modern Translations and Editions

In 1655, Edward Pococke published the Arabic text and Latin translations of the following parts of Maimonides' *Commentary on the Mishnah*:

1. General Introduction
2. Introduction of Chapter 10 (*Perek Chelek*) of tractate Sanhedrin
3. Introduction to tractate Avot, popularly known as "The Eight Chapters" or *Shemonah Perakim*
4. Introduction to Seder Kodashim
5. Introduction to tractate Menahot
6. Introduction to Seder Tohorot

Pococke's work is entitled *Porta Mosis Sive Dissertationes Aliquot A. R. Moses Maimonide. . . .* (Oxford, R. Davis Co.).

An excellent Latin translation of Maimonides' entire *Commentary on the Mishnah* in six volumes by the renowned Dutch scholar Wilhelm Surenhusius was pub lished in Amsterdam between 1698 and 1703 under the title *Mishna Sive Totius Hebraeorum Juris, rituum, Antiquitatum, ac Legum Oralium Systema, cum Clarissimorum Rabbinorum Maimonides et Bartenorae Commentarius Integris. . . .*

A new Hebrew translation of Seder Tohorot was published by Dr. J. Derenbourg in Berlin together with the Arabic text in three parts:

Part 1   appeared in Berlin in 1887 and contains the Introduction to Seder Tohorot and tractate Keilim.

Part 2   was completed in 1888 and contains tractates Oholot, Nega'im, and Parah.

Part 3   was published in 1889 and contains tractates Tohorot, Mikva'ot, Niddah, Makhshirin, Zavim, Tevul Yom, Yadayim, and Uktzin.

During the quarter century following Derenbourg's Hebrew translation of Seder Tohorot, many individual tractates were published in Europe as doctoral dissertations. Many of these were only parts of tractates and some were only editions of one or more *Mishnayot*. Most contained both Arabic text and a Hebrew translation. Annotations were in German, and an occasional tractate had a complete German translation. These were described in the periodical *Kiryat Sefer* by Abraham Yaari (Jerusalem, Vol. 9, 1932–1933,). pp.

101–109 and 228–235. The list is somewhat modified and amended as follows:

Seder Zera'im

Introduction	*Einleitung In Die Mischna*. Bernard Hamburger, Berlin, 1902.
Berakhot	*Der Commentar Des Maimuni' Zum Tractate Berachoth*, Ernst Weill, Berlin, 1891.
Pe'ah	*Mischna Commentar Zum Tractate Peah*. David Herzog, Berlin, 1894.
Demai	*Der Commentar Des Maimuni Zum Tractat Demai*, Joseph Zivi, Berlin, 1891.
Kilayim	*Maimuni's Commentar Zum Traktat Kilayim*, Salomon Bamberger, Frankfurt a.M., 1891.
Hallah	*Maimuni's Commentar Zum Traktat Challah*, Selig Bamberger, Frankfurt a.M., 1895.

Seder Mo'ed

Shabbat	*Der Mischna Commentar Des Maimonides Zum Tractat Moed Katan und Zum Tractat Shabbath*, V–VII. Jonas Simon, Berlin, 1902.
Shabbat	*Mischna Commentar Zum Tractat Sab-*

	bath, 8–12. Martinus Katz, Berlin, 1903.
Shabbat	*Mischna Commentar Zum Tractat Sabbath*, 13–18. Henricus Urbach, Budapest, 1904.
Shabbat	*Commentarius R. Mosis Maimuni in Mischnam ad Tractatum Sabbath.* Chaps. XIX, XXIV, Ludovicus Kohn, Budapest, 1903.
Eruvin	*Einige Bemerkungen Zum Maimuni's Mischnah Commentar des Tractats Erubin*, Chap. II, 5; VI, 2; VIII, 2. D. Grunewald. Monatsschr. Ges. Wiss. Juden. Vol. 44, pp. 452–454, 1900.
Pesahim	*Mischna Commentar Zum Tractat Pesachim*. Herman Kroner, Berlin, 1901.
Pesahim	*Maimonides' Commentary on the Mishnah in Arabic. Tractate Pesachim*, with a Hebrew translation. Rabbi Jacob Moses Toledano, Safed, 1915.
Shekalim	*Mischna Commentar Zum Tractat Shekalim*, 1–4. Joseph Borsodi, Budapest, 1904.
Shekalim	*Mischna Commentar Zum Tractat Shekalim*, 5–8. I. Diamant, Vienna, 1904.
Shekalim	*Maimonides Mishnah Commentary on Shekalim*, Chaps. 1–2. Rabbi Jacob

	Moses Toledano,Sinai (Jerusalem) Vol. 27, pp. 52–61, 1950.
Shekalim	*Maimonides Mishnah Commentary on Shekalim,* Chaps. 3–8. Rabbi Jacob Moses Toledano, Sinai (Jerusalem) Vol. 15, pp. 133–152, 1938.
Yoma	*Mischna Commentar Zum Tractat Joma,* 1–4. Emanuel Hirschfeld, Berlin, 1902.
Yoma	*Mischna Commentar Zum Tractat Yoma,* 5–8. Eug. Vidor, Budapest, 1904.
Yoma	*Maimonides Mischna Commentar. Yoma.* Boruch Toledano, Sinai (Jerusalem), Vol. 27, pp. 169–196; 288–310, 1950.
Sukkah	*Mischna Commentar Zum Tractat Sukkah,* Solomon Lovinger, Budapest, 1902.
Betzah	*Mischna Commentar Zum Tractat Bezah,* Herman Kroner, Munich, 1898.
Rosh Hashanah	*Maimonides Mischnah Commentary on Tractate Rosh Hashanah,* Chap. I, 1–2; Chap. III, 2 to the end of the tractate. M. S. L. Bamberger, Festschrift Zum 70 Geburtstage Von Dr. D. Hoffman, pp. 248–260, Berlin, 1914.

Rosh Hashanah	*Maimonides Mishnah Commentary on Tractate Rosh Hashanah*, Chaps. I, 3 to Chap. III, 1. M. Friedlander, Jubelschrift Zum 70 Geburtstage des Dr. Israel Hildesheimer, pp. 121–125, Berlin, 1890.
Taanit	*Mischna Commentar Zum Tractat Taanith*. Adolf Kallner, Leipzig, 1902.
Megillah	*Mischnah Commentar Zum Tractat Megillah*. Siegfried Behrens, Breslau, 1901.
Mo'ed Katan	*Der Mischna Commentar des Maimonides Zum Tractat Moed Katan und Zum Tractat Sabbath*, V–VII. Jonas Simon, Berlin, 1902.
Hagigah	*Mischna Commentar Zum Tractat Hagigah*. Artur Victor, Breslau, 1925.
Seder Nashim	
Ketubot	*Mischna Kommentar Zum Tractat Kethuboth*, I–II. Salomon Frankfurter, Berlin, 1903.
Ketubot	*Mischnah Kommentar Zum Tractat Kethuboth*, III–V. Moritz Frankfurter, Berlin, 1903.
Ketubot	*Maimonides Commentar Zum Tractat Kethuboth*, VI–VIII. Gottfried Freudman, Berlin, 1904.

Ketubot — *Mischnah Kommentar Zum Tractat Kethuboth*, IX–XI. Leopold Nebanzahl, Berlin, 1905.

Nazir — *Moses Maimonides Kommentar Zum Mischnah–Tractat Nazir*, I–IV. Friedrich Weiss, Berlin, 1906.

Gittin — *Maimuni's Commentar Zum Tractat Gittin*. Hirsch Goldberg, Berlin, 1902.

Sotah — *Mischna Commentar Zum Tractat Sota*, I–VI. Nathan Hoffman, Breslau, 1933.

Kiddushin — *Mischna Commentar Zum Tractat Kiddushin*. Aaron Nurock, Berlin, 1903.

Seder Nezikin

Bava Metzia — *Mischna Commentar Zum Tractat Baba Mezia*, 8–10. Jeshaja Silber, Wurzburg, 1925.

Bava Batra — *Mischna Commentar Zum Tractat Baba Bathra*, I–IV. Jacob Sanger, Berlin, 1912.

Bava Batra — *Mischna Commentar Zum Tractat Baba Bathra*, V–X. Emanuel Levy, Berlin, 1907.

Sanhedrin — *Mischna Commentar Zum Tractat Sanhedrin*, I–III. Moritz Weisz, Halle a.S., 1893.

Sanhedrin — *Maimonides Commentar Zum Tractat*

	Sanhedrin, IV–V. I. Bleichrode, Berlin, 1904.
Sanhedrin	*Maimonides Mishnah Commentary on Tractate Sanhedrin*, VI–VII. I. Bleichrode, Memorial Volume for Rabbi Isaac Kook, Vol. 3, pp. 3–43, 1937.
Sanhedrin	*Moses Maimuni's Einleitung Zu Chelek.* J. Holzer, Berlin, 1901.
Sanhedrin	*Introduction to Chapter Ten.* I Friedlander. In selections from the Arabic Writings of Maimonides. Brill, Leiden, 1909.
Sanhedrin	*Thirteen Principles of Faith*, Moses Guttstein. Tarbitz, Vol. 26.
Sanhedrin	*Maimuni's Commentar Zum Tractat Sanhedrin.* Manuel Gottlieb, Hanover, 1906.
Makkot	*Mischna Commentar Zum Tractat Makkoth.* J. Barth, Berlin, 1880.
Makkot/ Shevu'ot	*Mischna Commentar Zum Tractat Makkoth und Zum Tractat Shebuoth.* Manuel Gottlieb, Hanover, 1909.
Eduyot	*Maimonides Commentar Zum Tractat Edujoth*, 1, 1–12. M. Beerman, Berlin, 1897.
Eduyot	*Maimonides Kommentar Zum Tractat Eduyoth*, V–VI. Abraham A. Gorbate, Berlin, 1906.

Avodah Zarah	*Maimonides Commentar Zum Tractat Aboda Zara.* Joseph Wiener, Berlin, 1895.
Introduction to Avot	*Hesed Avraham*, A. Horowitz, Lublin, 1557.
Introduction to Avot	*Shemona Perakim*, Samuel Ibn Tibbon, Berlin, 1927.
Introduction to Avot	*Introduction to Tractate Aboth.* Maurice Wolff, Leipzig, 1863.
Introduction to Avot	*Introduction to Tractate Aboth.* Maurice Wolff. 2nd edition, Leiden, 1903.
Introduction to Avot	*Die Ethik des Maimonides oder Schemonah Perakim.* Simon Falkenheim, Konigsberg, 1832.
Introduction to Avot	*Der Commentar Des Maimonides Zu Den Spruchen der Vater.* M. Rawicz, Freiburg, 1910.
Avot	*Maimuni's Commentar Zu Tractat Aboth.* 1. E. Baneth. Jubelschrift Zum 70 Geburtstages des Dr. 1. Hildesheimer, Berlin, 1890.
Avot	*Maimuni's Commentar Zum Tractat Abot.* E. Baneth, Berlin, 1905.
Avot	*Perush LeMasechta Aboth.* M. Rabinowitz. Mossad Harav Kook, Jerusalem, 1961.
Avot	Many others too numerous to list here.

Seder Kodashim

Zevahim	*Maimuni's Commentar Zum Tractat Zebachim.* (Only several passages) J. Derenbourg. In Kavod Halvanon Year 6 #11.
Hullin	*Maimuni's Commentar Zum Tractat Chulin*, III–IV. Moses Wohl, Berlin, 1894.
Bekhorot	*Maimonides Commentar Zum Tractat Bechoroth.* Julius Lowenstein, Berlin, 1897.
Arakhin	*Maimuni's Commentar Zum Tractat Arachim.* Israel Shapiro, Jerusalem, 1910.
Me'ilah	*Maimonides Commentar Zum Tractat Meilah*, 1–111. Rabbi David Carelbach, Cologne, 1923–1924.
Tamid	*Maimonides Commentar Zum Tractat Tamid.* Moses Fried, Frankfurt a.M, 1903.
Middot	*Maimonides Commentar Zum Tractat Middoth.* Jacob Fromer, Breslau, 1898.

Seder Tohorot

Keilim	*Commentary on the Mishnah, Tractate Kelim.* Judah Edel, Bialystok, 1816.

The Entire   J. Derenbourg. (See description
Seder   above.) The only parts of the Com-
                 mentary that have ever been trans-
                 lated into English are:

1. The Introduction to Chapter 10 of tractate Sanhedrin. *Maimonides on the Jewish Creed.* J. Abelson.
   Jewish Quarterly Review, 1906–1907, Vol. 19,
   pp. 24–58.
2. The Introduction to Tractate Abot. *The Eight
   Chapters of Maimonides on Ethics.* Joseph I. Gorfinkle. New York, Columbia University Press,
   1912, pp. 104 (Eng) and 55 (Heb).
3. *The Commentary to Mishnah Aboth.* Arthur David.
   New York, Bloch Publishing Co., 1968, pp. xxi
   and 166.

Recently, Rabbi Joseph David Kafich in Israel re-
translated the entire commentary from Arabic into
Hebrew using heretofore unknown Arabic manuscripts uncovered in Yemen after several centuries, in
addition to the known extant manuscripts in the libraries of Western Europe and the Middle East. Seder
Zera'im (1963), Seder Mo'ed (1964), Seder Nezikin
(1965), Seder Nashim (1965), Seder Kodashim (1967),
and Seder Tohorot (1968) were published by Mossad
Harav Kook in Jerusalem in both the original Arabic
and new Hebrew translation.

Also available are innumerable commentaries on

Maimonides' *Commentary on the Mishnah*. It would be impossible to give a complete bibliography of these here, nor is it germane to the current work.

One should further not confuse Maimonides' Commentary on certain tractates of the Gemara with his *Commentary on the Mishnah*.

The Current Edition

With the exception of several isolated segments of Maimonides' *Commentary on the Mishnah* that were translated into German, the introduction to and tractate Avot, and the tenth chapter of tractate Sanhedrin, which were translated into English as described above, Maimonides Commentary has not been published in a Western language and thus this work has only been available to the Hebrew or Arabic reader. The current edition represents the translation into English of Maimonides' long introduction to his *Commentary on the Mishnah*.

In the present volume, the Hebrew text is that of the standard published Mishnah text, which is nearly identical with that found in all copies of the Vilna edition of the Babylonian Talmud. Where slight differences between these exist, it is so noted.

In the translation of Maimonides' Introduction to his Commentary proper, the major source work used was the Hebrew translation of Kafich.

INTRODUCTION

A few words regarding the philosophy of translation in general seem appropriate here. There are two major types of translations. One is where an attempt is made to render as closely as possible the flavor and sense of the original work. The other type of translation is where one tries in a loose manner to present the content of the original work, but where one uses the syntax and style of the language into which one is translating. The present translation attempts to follow the former philosophy.

Medieval Hebrew writing is unique in that it uses a style in which subordinate clauses, apposites, and the like are not systematically handled according to rules of grammar. In medieval Hebrew, thoughts are written as they come to the mind of the writer without distinction between main clauses, subordinate clauses, and digressions, and without modifiers. Thus, Maimonides not infrequently presents a thought, veers off into a lengthy digression, and returns to the original idea, without making clear where the digression begins and ends.

Another general comment concerns the Hebrew language itself. Medieval Hebrew is not the same as biblical Hebrew, nor is it the same as modern Hebrew. A word may have several meanings in biblical Hebrew yet only one connotation or a single shade of meaning of this word is intended in medieval Hebrew. For example, the Hebrew word *Emunah* in modern Hebrew means faith, in medieval Hebrew means integrity, and in biblical Hebrew connotes either or both. Faith and integrity are not identical meanings of the word *Emunah*. In the present translation, the proper meaning that Maimonides intended was selected to render a word or phrase into English, although this shade of meaning may differ from the modern or biblical sense of the word or phrase. Occasionally, when Maimonides' intent is not clear, alternative meanings are given.

The major purpose of this English translation is to bring to the non-Hebrew and non-Arabic reading public the wisdom and genius of the medieval giant of Judaism, Moses Maimonides. Therefore, a precise word by word translation is unnecessary and even undesirable, since it would make the reading difficult and possibly even unintelligible. Maimonides himself, writing to his friend and most renowned translator Rabbi Samuel Ibn Tibbon, stated that a translator should attempt to translate the meaning of an original work rather than offer an incomprehensible word by word translation. In this light, the current translation attempts to remain as literal as possible and yet retain and impart all of Maimonides' original thoughts and ideas.

Quotations from the Mishnah are printed in capital letters. Scriptural quotations are in italics. An occasional word or phrase in brackets is added to facilitate understanding of the text but is not present in the original.

MAIMONIDES'
INTRODUCTION
TO HIS
COMMENTARY
ON THE
MISHNAH

Gather[1] ye Sages and take your positions[2]
For I will present you with a pleasing gift;
Come ye children, hearken unto me
I will teach you the fear of the Lord.[3]
Hearken diligently unto Me and eat that which is good[4]
That your souls may be as a succulent garden.
Who is the man that desireth life
And loveth days, that he may see good therein[5]
Who has not accepted the great king's yoke[6]
Nor cowered before Him
Nor has he fallen prey to the temptations thereof

But he purposed in his heart that he would not
   defile himself with the king's food or wine[7]
Let him stop here for the feast that I have
   prepared
And partake of the wine that I have poured
And join the table that I have arranged
Come eat of my bread and drink of the wine
   which I have mixed[8]
Behold, it contains all types of precious fruit
Fresh as well as old;[9]
And the spiced wine of pomegranate juice[10]
That gently moves the lips of those that
   sleep;[11]
It represents the heave offering of my wine
And the first fruits of my produce,[12]
My threshing and the winnowing of my
   floor,[13]
And that wine is of the "vineyard of Ben
   Shemen"[14]
And its bread is the bread of the mighty[15]
Smooth and fat to whosoever eats a portion
   thereof
And its taste is as the taste of fresh oil.[16]
Eat of the richness and drink of the sweetness,
   my sons;[17]
Eat friends, drink abundantly,[18] my
   understanding ones;

This is the table that is before the Lord.[19]

It is a Commentary on the Mishnah; (that
   Mishnah) which your forefathers
   propounded

And it is an explanation of the fences that the
   shepherds erected[20]

The leaders who cared for the weanlings.[21]

And it[22] presents fundamentals of the principles
   that are your foundations

And the customs, the decrees and the
   ordinances

That your great ones[23] prescribed

From the day that the Lord gave
   commandment

And onward throughout your generations.[24]

Behold, it is as the Tower of David standing
   on its hills

Whereupon there hang a thousand shields[25]

Together with the weapons of war of the
   strong,[26]

All the armor of the mighty men.[27]

I, MOSES THE SON OF MAIMON THE
   SPANIARD have built it[28]

And from the ocean of the Talmud did I draw
   it

And from the gems of the *Tosefta* did I solidify
   its foundation

And with the glittering stones of the *Sifra* did I
　　set its base
And with the gold of the *Sifri* did I lay its
　　plaster
And I have buttressed it with the words of the
　　Gaonim[29]
And, as purified silver have I refined it
And into the depths of my heart have I poured
　　it.
Behold, it is as a cherished vineyard
And as a delightful plant have I sown it
By day and by night have I guarded it
And at intervals irrigated it
Until its blossoms bloomed and its grape
　　clusters ripened.
And now every blossom has opened
And each tree therein has flourished
And the mandrakes emit a fragrance.
I have opened its gates and have not bolted
　　them.
Neither by day nor by night did I close it
And to all righteous and honest have I brought
　　it
And as a gift to the studious have I sent it.
Behold, I have forbidden it to all who copy
　　words.

To those that dwell before the Lord shall it be
To eat their fill and for stately clothing.[30]

Every[31] commandment that the Holy One,
Blessed be He, gave to Moses our Teacher, may he
rest in peace,[32] was given with its clarification. First
He told him the commandment and then He expounded on its explanation and content, including
all that which is included in the Torah. The manner
of its transmittal to Israel occurred as stated in the
Gemara:[33] Moses entered into the Tent, and first
Aaron entered unto him. Moses then stated to him
a single time the commandment he had received,
and taught him its explanation, following which
Aaron retreated to the right of Moses.

Thereupon, Elazar and Itamar, Aaron's sons,
entered and Moses told them what he had told
Aaron, and then they stepped back. One sat to the
left of Moses, and the other on the right of Aaron.
Then the seventy Elders entered, and Moses
taught them, just as he had taught Aaron and his
sons. Following this came the masses of people,
every one seeking God, and Moses spoke to them
so that all had heard it directly from him. The
result is that Aaron heard that precept from Moses
four times, his sons three times, the Elders twice,

and the remainder of the populace once. Moses then left and Aaron repeated that commandment that he had learned, having heard it from Moses four times as we have mentioned, to all those present. Aaron then also left, so that his sons had also heard the precept four times; three times from Moses, and once from Aaron. After Aaron had departed, Elazar and Itamar repeated and taught that commandment that they had heard four times to the entire populace that was present, and then ceased their teaching. Thus we find that the seventy Elders heard the precept four times: twice from Moses, once from Aaron, and once from Elazar and Itamar. The Elders themselves then repeated and expounded that commandment to the populace once and, thus, we find that the entire congregation heard the precept in question four times: once from Moses, once from Aaron, a third time from his sons, and the fourth time from the Elders. After this, all the people went to teach one another what they had heard from Moses and to write that commandment on scrolls. The leaders roamed over all of Israel to [insure that the people] learn and apply themselves until they understood that commandment and were fluent in reading it. They would then teach them the explanation of that God-given precept. That explanation would include all aspects, and they would write the precept and learn by heart the oral tradition.[34]

Thus, our Sages, of blessed memory, said: the Written Law and the Oral Law.

Thus, our Sages, of blessed memory, said in the *Beraita*:[35] *And the Lord spoke unto Moses at Mount Sinai.*[36] Why does the teaching state specifically at Mount Sinai? Was not the entire Torah given[37] at Sinai? The reason is to tell us that just as the law of *Shemitah*[38] was stated with its generalities, specifics, and fine details at Sinai, so too all the commandments were stated with their generalities, specifics, and fine details at Sinai. You have an example of this when the Holy One, Blessed be He, told Moses: *Ye shall dwell in booths for seven days,*[39] following which He informed him that this *sukkah*[40] is an obligation upon males and not females, and that sick people are not so obligated, nor travelers; also the covering of the *sukkah* should only be of that which grows from the earth, and that one should not use wool or silk or utensils for a covering even when these utensils are made of products which grow from the earth, such as mats, and clothing. [God also clearly indicated that] eating, drinking and sleeping therein are all obligatory for the entire seven days [of *Sukkot*]. Furthermore, its interior space should not be less than seven handbreadths in length by seven handbreadths in width, nor shall the height [of the *Sukkah*] be less than ten handbreadths. And when the prophet [Moses], may he rest in peace, came, he received this commandment with its explanation, and so too all the 613 precepts with their explanations; the commandment in writing, and the explanation by oral transmission.

And it came to pass in the fortieth year, in the eleventh month[41] on the day of the New Moon of the month of Shevat, that Moses gathered the people and told them: *The time of my death has arrived. If there is any one among you who heard a law and forgot it, let him come and ask me and I will explain it. Also, let anyone to whom a question remains in doubt come and I will clarify it* as it is written: *Moses began to explain this Torah saying. . . .*[42] Thus too did the Sages state in *Sifre*:[43] "Let he who has forgotten [even] one single law come and relearn it and whoever is in need of explanation, let him come and it will be explained."[44] From Moses' mouth they received clarification of the law and learned the explanations during the entire period, from the New Moon of Shevat until the seventh of Adar.[45] When he was close to death he began to write the Torah on scrolls,[46] and he wrote thirteen Torah scrolls, all of rolled parchment, from the letter *Bet* of *Bereishit*[47] to the last *Lamed* of *L'einei Kol Yisrael*.[48] He gave one scroll to each tribe to conduct itself according to its laws. He gave the thirteenth scroll to the Levites and told them: *Take this book of the law*,[49] after which he ascended the Mount at noon[50] of the seventh day[51] of the month of Adar, as tradition has deduced.[52] We would consider that process to be death, because he was taken from us. However, he lives in the glory of the height to which he ascended.[53] So too is it stated "Moses our Teacher, did not die; rather he ascended and is serving in heaven."[54] Discussions of these matters are extremely lengthy, and this is not the place to expound upon them.

He died, may he rest in peace, after having bequeathed to Joshua the explanations that were given to him. And Joshua and the people of his generation studied them. And of all that he or one of the Elders received from Moses, there was no need for further discussion, since no disagreement occurred thereon. And that which they did not hear directly from the prophet [Moses], of blessed memory, required discussion and deliberation, the decision in a given case being derived by means of reasoning[55] or by means of the thirteen principles given at Mount Sinai, which are the thirteen principles through which the Torah may be expounded.[56] Some of these interpreted laws were free of argumentation, everyone agreeing [to a single view]. On some of them, however, differences of opinion occurred between two views, the one ruling thusly and the other thusly, the former deducing his view and, by means of reason, strengthening it in his own mind, and the latter also presenting reason to strengthen his opinion. It is because of the analysis by analogy[57] or by means of reasoning that this difference in their opinions occurs. And when such a difference of opinion occurs, one follows the ruling of the majority as it is written: *Thou shalt follow the majority.*[58]

Know, too, that prophecy is not helpful in the interpretation of the Torah, nor in the study of the laws through the thirteen principles. Rather, that which Joshua and Pinchas wrought was [not through prophecy but] through deliberation and logical derivation, much the same as did Ravina and Rav Ashi.[59] The advantage of a prophet and his accomplishment in the matter of any commandment, if you inquire into this, is, by my life,[60] among the great principles upon which the faith is supported and founded.

I see that this is an appropriate point to explain this fundamental subject [of prophecy]. This cannot be done until we have analyzed the claim of the prophet to his prophecy, and whereby the prophecy is corroborated since this, too, is a fundamental principle. The great masses of people, as well as a number of learned individuals among them, are under a false impression in assuming[61] that prophecy cannot be attributed to one claiming it unless[62] he has performed a wondrous miracle,[63] such as one of the miracles of Moses, or if he changes the course of nature as when Elijah brought back to life the son of the widow[64] or, as is known to all, the miracles of Elisha.[65] This is not a correct principle, because all the miracles which Elijah, Elisha, and other prophets wrought were not performed in order to substantiate their prophecy, since their prophethood had already been established previously; rather they performed these wonders for their own needs. Because of their closeness to the Holy One, Blessed be He, He fulfilled their desires, just as He promised the righteous: *Thou shalt decree a thing and it will be fulfilled unto thee.*[66] Prophethood becomes established in the manner I will begin to discuss. First let me state that the fundamental principle of our faith in the matter of prophecy is as follows: Those who claim to be prophets can first be divided into two categories, namely they who prophesy in the name of idolatry, and those who prophesy in the name of God.

The prophecy in the name of idolatry is subdivided into two categories: the first category is if a prophet should arise and say "that particular star set its spirit upon me and told me 'Worship me thusly' or 'Call unto me thusly.' " Similarly, if he should call people to worship an idol or any image or shape saying "This [image] apprised me of such and such, and told me thusly," or "commanded me to cause it to be worshiped in such and such a way," in the manner of the prophets of *Baal* and of the prophets of *Asherah*.[67] [These are false prophets.]

The second category is if someone should say: "A vision of God came to me to worship a particular idol," or "to call down such and such a heavenly power in such and such a manner." He will teach the people matters pertaining to the worship or activities of that particular form of idolatry, as the Torah has described.[68] This type [of prophecy, using God's name] is also considered prophecy in the name of idolatry, because this latter appellation includes both the person who states that the idol itself commanded him to worship it as well as He who states that the Holy One, Blessed be He, commanded him to worship any created being.

Should one of the two claims just described become heard from one who pretends to be a prophet, and should witnesses testify according to the laws of the Torah,[69] his punishment is death by strangulation as the Holy One, Blessed be He, stated: *And that prophet or that dreamer of dreams shall be put to death.*[70] We should not examine his pretention to prophecy, nor should we ask him for a miracle. Even if he should perform more wondrous miracles than we have ever heard of to establish his prophecy, he should nevertheless be punished by strangulation. One should pay no attention to those miracles,[71] because the reason for the occurrence of such miracles is as stated in Scriptures: *For the Lord your God is testing you.*[72] For the testimony of the intellect that belies his prophecy is more reliable than the evidence of the eye which sees his miracles, because it is clear to intelligent people that one should not honor or worship save the One who brings forth all that exists,[73] and the One who is alone in perfection [i.e., God].

Those who prophesy in the name of God are also subdivided into two categories:

The first category includes one who prophesies in the name of the Lord, and calls upon the populace to believe in Him and preaches regarding His worship saying that the Holy One, Blessed be He, added a precept to His commandments, or deleted one from the sum total of those commandments that are included in the Torah. There is no difference if he[74] adds to or deletes from that which is written in the scriptural text, or whether he adds to or deletes from the accepted interpretation thereof. The concept of adding to or deleting from a biblical text is exemplified by his saying, "The Holy One, Blessed be He, told me that *Orlah*[75] applies only for two years, and after two years it is permitted for you to eat from newly planted fruits," or if he should say, "The Holy One, Blessed be He, told me that *Orlah* is forbidden to be eaten until four years have passed," instead of what the Holy One, Blessed be He, really said: *Three years shall it be as forbidden*[76] *unto you; it shall not be eaten,*[77] and the like. Another example is related to modification of anything learned through tradition, even if the apparent meaning of the text should support him, such as if he should say that the biblical phrase *And thou shalt cut off her hand*[78] means literally to hew off her hand rather than meaning monetary compensation for the shame she caused, as is the traditional interpretation, and support his claim to prophecy saying: "The Holy One, Blessed be He, told me that this commandment which states '*And thou shalt cut off her hand'* should be taken literally." Such a person should also be killed by strangulation, because he is a false prophet and attributes to the Holy One, Blessed be He, things that He never told him. Here too one should pay no heed to the sign or miracle of such a person, because the prophet [Moses] who showed his miracles to all the people of the world and instilled God in our hearts and His truth and belief in Him as it is written in Scriptures: *And they will also believe in Thee forever,*[79] related to us in the name of the Holy One, Blessed be He, that no other Torah shall ever come from God save this one. And this is what is meant by *It is not in Heaven . . .*[80] and *It is in thy mouth and thy heart to perform it.*[81] *In thy mouth* refers to scriptural phrases that are well known to you. *In thy heart* refers to laws deduced by logical derivation through study, which is one of the powers attributed to the heart. He also warned us against adding to them[82] or deleting from them as it is written: *Thou shalt not add thereto nor substract from it.*[83] For this reason the Sages, of blessed memory, stated: "No prophet may introduce any new law hereafter."[84] And since we know from his words that he spoke falsely about the Holy One, Blessed be He, and attributed to Him that which He never told him, we are obligated to kill him, as written in Scripture: *And the prophet who will intentionally speak a word in My name which I have not commanded him to speak, or who shall speak in the name of other gods, that prophet shall die.*[85]

The second category is exemplified by a prophet who calls people to worship God, commanding them to obey His precepts and exhorting them to observe the Torah without addition or deletion, as the last of the prophets stated: *Remember Ye the Law of Moses, my servant, which I commanded unto him in Horeb for all Israel, statutes and ordinances.*[86] He further assures rewards to those who comply, and warns all who would transgress it, of punishment, as did Isaiah, Jeremiah, Ezekiel, and others. He also prescribes ordinances, and decrees prohibitions on a subject that is not in the Torah, such as if he says, "Wage war with such and such a town or people now," as Samuel commanded Saul to wage war with Amalek,[87] or, conversely, if he preaches abstention from killing, as Elisha did when he prevented Yehoram[88] from smiting the soldiers of Haza'el who had entered the city of Samaria, according to the well-known story[89] or as Isaiah prevented the bringing of water inside the city wall,[90] or as Jeremiah prevented the Jews from leaving Jerusalem,[91] and similar instances. For this reason, if a prophet claims that his statements are prophetic, and does not connect them with idolatry, nor does he add to the Torah, nor delete from it, but says different things, such as we have just described, we are not required to investigate him to ascertain the veracity of his claim,[92] for we must obey anything commanded by one whose prophetic claim is verified, from the smallest to the greatest task. Whosoever fails to fulfill any of his[93] commands is culpable of death by Divine agency,[94] as the Holy One, Blessed be He, stated regarding him who transgresses a command of a prophet: *I will require [the penalty for] it from him.*[95] However, should the prophet's claim not be substantiated, then he must die by strangulation. The substantiation of a prophet's claim is achieved as I shall presently describe: if a person claims prophethood, as we have explained, and he is fit for it, that is, if he is a man of learning, integrity,[96] temperance, wisdom, and pleasant traits, as it is fundamental to us that prophecy cannot rest upon any other save a man who is wise, strong, and rich.[97] There are many details regarding this subject of prophecy, and it is impossible to collect them all together here. Discussions thereon and proof for each one are to be found in verses of the books of the Torah and in the words of the Sages and elsewhere. This subject would require an entire book in itself. Perhaps God will help us in compiling what is appropriate in a book on that subject.

Should now the prophet be eligible to prophesy[98] and begins to prophesy, we tell him to provide us assurances and inform us of specific things which the Holy One, Blessed be He, told him. He will then relate these to us. Should all his predictions become fulfilled, we will know that his prophecy is true. Should he falsify any of his statements, even on a minor point, we will know that he is a false prophet. This type of examination procedure is written in the Torah: *And if thou say in thine heart, how shall we know the word that God has not spoken; that which the prophet will speak in the name of the Lord and the thing will not follow nor come to pass.*[99] Even if his words become verified on the basis of one or two assurances, his prophecy is still not necessarily absolutely substantiated; rather, his prophethood should be kept in abeyance until the truth of all that he speaks in God's name is verified, time after time. For this reason it states in the case of Samuel, when it became well-known and clear that everything that he said would come about: *And All Israel from Dan even unto Beer Sheba knew that Samuel was truly a prophet of the Lord.*[100] In all matters they consulted with prophets. Were it not for this consultation with prophets on all matters, Saul would not have come to Samuel to question him regarding that which he had lost at the beginning of the story.[101] There is no question that this is correct, because the Holy One, Blessed be He, established prophets for us to answer all our questions in place of astrologers,[102] enchanters and diviners, to enable us to question them [the prophets] in all matters regarding generalities and specifics. They give us true answers according to the word of God just as those diviners relate things that may or may not come true, as it is written: *For these nations which thou shalt possess hearken unto sorcerers and unto diviners but not so thou, the Eternal thy God has not suffered thee to do so. A prophet from thy midst from thy brethren like myself [will the Lord your God establish unto thee. Unto him shall ye hearken].*[103] Because of these facts, a prophet was called "Seer," because he foresaw the future before it happened as it is written: *For he that is today called a prophet was before time called a seer.*[104]

Should anyone think to himself and say that if prophethood is established by the fulfillment of the prediction of future events by him who makes such claims, then all the enchanters, astrologers, and spiritualists[105] could plead a claim of prophecy, since we often observe them predicting what the future will bring. By my life,[106] this is a vast topic, and it is worthy of explanation, in order to clarify the difference between the words of him who prophesies in the name of the Lord, and the words of these spiritualists. I say that the enchanters, astrologers, and other people in that category do predict future happenings, but only some predictions will be right, and some will be definitely false. This we see constantly, and even the performers of such an art agree to this, and do not deny it.[107] They pride themselves in the fact that the false predictions of one of them are fewer than those of others; but for any one to be correct in all details [of his predictions] is impossible. Even these spiritualists do not claim to be [correct in all aspects of the things they foretell]; rather they say that this year will be one of drought and that no rain will fall at all, and yet a little rain does fall; or one of them might say that tomorrow it will rain and yet rain does not fall until the day after tomorrow, and the like. This only happens in the case of one who is very expert or very renowned, and of whom it is written in astrological books. This is the idea of the words of Isaiah to Babylon: *Let now the astrologers, the stargazers and the monthly prognosticators stand up and save thee from the things that shall come upon thee,*[108] and our Sages pointed out that [the verse] is *from the* and not *all the.*[109]

Not so the prediction of true prophets; their promises prove to be correct to the very end. Never does even one item, small or large, of their statements ever fail, of that which they speak in the name of the Lord. Thus, if any of his[110] words should be unsustained,[111] then we know his fraudulence [as a divine prophet]. This, too, is written: *There shall not fail anything of the word of the Lord.*[112] This, also, is what Jeremiah alluded to in reference to dreamers who may have been correct in their visions, and who profess that what they see in dreams is by way of prophecy. He reproved them and demolished their claims by saying: *The prophet that hath a dream, let him tell a dream; and that hath My word, let him speak My word truthfully. What hath the chaff [straw] to do with the grain [wheat]? saith the Lord.*[113] The Sages explained this matter saying that prophecy is clear and has no falsehoods mixed in, as pure grain that has been separated from the chaff. Dreams and the like of magicians are mixed with falsehood, like straw that has a few grains of wheat in it. They further stated: "Just as wheat cannot be without straw, so there cannot be a dream without some nonsensical parts."[114]

There is one important remaining notion which is worthy of clarification at this point. It refers to a prophet who predicts evil events that will befall the people of which they are deserving, such as if he warns them regarding famine, or destruction by the sword, or of an earthly upheaval, or that hailstones will fall upon them, and the like, and afterward none of these things come to pass because Heaven forgave them and their condition remains one of tranquility. One cannot conclude from this the falsehood of such a prophet, nor can one say he is a false prophet and that he is liable to the death penalty, because the Holy One, Blessed be He, repented from doing harm. It is also possible that they[115] did penance and turned from their provocative acts, or that the Holy One, Blessed be He, deferred their punishment in His compassion and postponed His ire toward them until a later date,[116] as He did to Ahab in His statement through Elijah: *I will not bring the evil in his days, but in his son's days will I bring the evil.*[117] Or He may have forgiven them[118] because of previous merits on their part.

[The scriptural phrase] *And the thing does not follow nor come to pass*[119] was not said for this type of example; rather it refers to the following: if he assures us that good tidings will occur at a specific time saying "In this year there will be tranquility and contentment," and then wars occurred, or if he says "This year will be one of rain and abundance," and then famine and drought occurred, and the like, then we know that he is a false prophet, and the falsehood and untruth of his claim will be clearly established. Concerning this does Scripture state: *The prophet has spoken presumptuously, thou shalt not be afraid of him*[120] meaning that his faith, his honesty, and his wisdom should not frighten you, nor terrify you of killing him, after he dared[121] to testify about such a serious matter and spoke falsehood about the Lord, Blessed be He. For when the Holy One, Blessed be He, promises good tidings to a people through a prophet, He certainly[122] fulfills them in order to establish his prophethood to the people. This is what the Sages, of blessed memory, meant when they said: "Every word of blessing that issues from the mouth of the Holy One, Blessed be He, even if conditional, is never withdrawn by Him."[123] Yet we find an account of the fear of Jacob after the Holy One, Blessed be He, assured him of good tidings, as it is written: *And behold I am with thee and will watch over thee whithersoever thou goest,*[124] and he feared lest he die, as it is written *And Jacob feared greatly and was distressed.*[125] The Sages, of blessed memory, say that the fear refers to the fear of serious sin, lest it cause him to perish, and this is what the Sages meant when they stated: "He thought that some sin might be the cause [of the failure] of God's promise to be fulfilled."[126] This tells us that the Holy One, Blessed be He, may promise good, and then sins prevail so that the good does not become fulfilled. One should know that this is only a matter between the Holy One, Blessed be He, and the prophet.

However, far be it for the Holy One, Blessed be He, to tell a prophet to assure the people of a good tiding unconditionally and then for this good not to become fulfilled. Such a thing cannot be because there would not exist for us any way to establish the authenticity of the prophecy. The Holy One, Blessed be He, gave us in His Torah the fundamental principle that a prophet is proven when his assurances become realized.[127] This important theme was implied by Jeremiah in his argument with Hananiah,[128] the son of Azzur, because Jeremiah prophesied evil and death saying that Nebuchadnezzar would prevail and conquer and destroy the Holy Temple, whereas Hananiah, the son of Azzur, predicted good, and predicted the return to Jerusalem of the vessels of the Lord's House that had been taken to Babylon.[129] To this

Jeremiah answered in this argumentation with him,[130] applying these traditional fundamental principles saying: *If my prophecy will not be established and if Nebuchadnezzar will not be victorious and if the vessels will be returned to the House of the Lord as you are saying, then this would not constitute a denial of my prophecy since perhaps the Holy One, Blessed be He, will have mercy upon them.*[131] *However, if your words will not become fulfilled and if the vessels will not be returned to the House of the Lord, then, as a result, it will become clear that your prophecy is false. Your prophethood will not become established until the good times that you promise will become fulfilled.* This is what he[132] meant when he also stated: *Nevertheless hear thou now this word that I speak in thine ears and in the ears of all the people. The prophets that have been in the world before me and before thee prophesied to many countries and of great kingdoms, of war and of evil and of pestilence. The prophet that prophesieth of peace, when the word of the prophet shall come to pass, then shall the prophet be known, that the Lord hath truly sent him.*[133] By this he meant that, concerning those prophets who prophesy for good and for evil, we do not know of all the things they prophesy for evil, whether their testimony is authentic or contrived. However, the truth of their words becomes known if they promise good and it becomes fulfilled.

If the prophecy of a prophet is fulfilled according to the principles we have just established, and he becomes renowned like Samuel and Elijah and others, that prophet has the right to do something in the Torah that no other living person can, as I will explain. If he dictates to abolish any precept of the positive commandments or if he decrees to permit any forbidden thing of the negative commandments[134] [*temporarily*, due to special circumstances], it is incumbent upon us to listen to all his words. And anyone who transgresses this command is culpable of death by divine decree,[135] except [if the prophet preaches] idolatry. The latter is a statement of the Sages in the Talmud: "In every matter, if a prophet tells you to transgress the commands of the Torah, obey him, with the exception of idolatry."[136] This rule applies only on condition that his decree should not be a permanent one and that he not say that the Holy One, Blessed be He, commanded to do thus and thus for all generations; rather he decreed to abolish this law temporarily for a good reason. The prophet himself should be asked regarding his order to transgress one of the precepts that God commanded us through Moses, and should answer that the suspension of that command will not be permanent but should be obeyed at present only, temporarily, just as the Court[137] would decree [a ruling] for a limited time period.

This is what Elijah did on Mount Carmel when he sacrificed a burnt offering outside the Temple[138] at a time when the Holy Temple was already built in Jerusalem. Anyone who performs this type of activity without prophetic command is culpable of *Karet,*[139] and the Holy One, Blessed be He, warned us of this in the Torah saying: *take heed to thyself lest thou offer thy burnt offerings in every place that thou seest.*[140] He who acts in this manner shall be culpable of divine punishment,[141] as it is written concerning him who offers a sacrifice outside the sanctuary: *Blood shall be imputed unto that man, he hath shed blood; and that man shall be cut off from among his people.*[142] If Elijah would have been asked at the time of his offering on Mount Carmel, and had we said to him, "Can we do such as this deed for all times?" he would have answered that it is prohibited and whosoever brings an offering outside the sanctuary is culpable of divine punishment, but this action was taken only for now to reveal thereby the falsity of the prophets of the *Baal,* and to thwart their activities.[143]

This concept is also exemplified by what Elisha did when he commanded the people to wage war with Moab, and to destroy fruit-bearing trees as it is written: *And every good tree shall ye fell*,[144] although God restrained us from doing so when He stated: *"Thou shalt not destroy the trees thereof by forcing an ax against them."*[145] If Elisha would have been asked whether this commandment was eradicated, and whether it would be permitted for us in the future to destroy fruit-bearing trees when we besiege a city, he would have answered that it is prohibited, and the act that he performed was done out of momentary necessity.

I will now bring you an example to clarify this fundamental principle applicable to all commandments. If a prophet whose prophethood was clearly verified to us, as we have described above, should tell us on the Sabbath that we should all rise, men and women alike, light a fire, and fashion therewith weapons of war, gird the weapons and wage war with the people of such and such a place on this day, which is the Sabbath, plunder their spoils, and conquer their women, it would be obligatory upon us—we who are bound[146] by the Torah of Moses—to immediately rise and comply. We should not delay in that which we are commanded, and should zealously and diligently perform that which he[147] has instructed us, without any hesitation, and without procrastination. We should firmly believe in all that we do on that day, even though it is the Sabbath and we are lighting a fire and doing work and killing and waging war, all of which are commands [through the prophet from God]. For this we hope for a goodly reward from the Holy One, Blessed be He, for having complied with the command of the prophet, because it is a positive commandment to observe his word as God commanded us through Moses: *A prophet from the midst of thee, of thy brethren, like me, will the Lord Thy God raise unto thee; unto him shall ye hearken.*[148] This is traditionally interpreted: "In every matter if a prophet tells you to transgress the commands of the Torah, obey him, with the exception of idolatry."[149] Thus, for example, if he tells us, "Worship this particular idol for this day only," or "Sacrifice[150] to this particular star at such and such a time," he should be killed and not listened to.

If a man considers in his heart that he is righteous and God-fearing, and if he is old and advanced in years and says: "Behold, I am very old and have lived so and so many years and have never transgressed a single precept of all the commandments of the Torah. How can I now rise on this day which is the Sabbath and transgress a prohibition, the penalty for which is death by stoning, and go to wage war? I will not add nor delete [from the commandments], and others may be found in place of me, and there are many people to accomplish this task."[151] Such a man is transgressing against the word of God, and is culpable of death by heavenly decree,[152] because he is transgressing the command of the prophet. He who commanded us to observe the Sabbath is the same One who commanded us to obey the words of the prophet and his decree. Whosoever transgresses his precept is guilty, as we have just mentioned. This is the meaning of the scriptural verse: *And it shall be that whosoever will not hearken unto My words which he[153] shall speak in My name, I will require it of him.*[154]

However, he who ties a permanent knot[155] on that Sabbath day while performing these tasks and does not need the knot as an aid in the fulfillment of the command that the prophet instructed is culpable of death by stoning. Should the prophet himself who commanded us what he did on that Sabbath, whose order we complied with, now claim that the Sabbath limits[156] are two thousand cubits minus one cubit, or two thousand cubits plus one cubit, and if he attributes this statement as having been told to him by way of prophecy and not derived through deduction and reasoning, then he is a false prophet and shall die by strangulation. In this manner should you evaluate everything a prophet may command you, and all that you find in Scriptures regarding a prophet who contradicts any precept of the commandments of the Torah. This principle is the key to this whole subject. In this alone does a prophet differ from other people in the matter of commandments. However, regarding deduction, reasoning and understanding of Torah commandments, he is as all other Sages who have no prophethood. That is to say, if a prophet should offer an opinion, and if a non-prophet should reason [a differing] opinion, and if the prophet should say "The Holy One, Blessed be He, told me that my conclusion is the correct one," one should not listen to him. Even if a thousand prophets, all of the stature of Elijah or Elisha would hold one opinion, and one thousand and one Sages would hold the opposite opinion, one must follow the majority,[157] and the final ruling is in accordance with the one thousand and one Sages, and not in accordance with the one thousand honored prophets. So too did our Sages state: "By God, even if Joshua, the son of Nun, had told it to me by his own mouth, I would not have accepted it."[158] They further stated: "If Elijah should come and declare that *Halitzah*[159] may be performed with a shoe,[160] he would be obeyed; with a sandal,[161] he would not be obeyed."[162]

Thus, they mean to say that under no circumstances can one add to or delete from a Torah precept through prophecy. So, too, if a prophet claims that the Holy One, Blessed be He, told him that the final law concerning that commandment is so and so, and that the opinion of so and so is correct, such a prophet shall be killed because he is a false prophet, as we established above. This is because no Torah was given after the first prophet,[163] and one may not add to nor delete from it as it is written: *It is not in heaven. . . .*[164]

The Holy One, Blessed be He, did not permit us to learn from prophets; rather from the Sages—people of deductive reasoning. It is not written "And thou shalt come to the prophet that shall be in those days"; rather *And thou shalt come unto the priests, the Levites and unto the Judge that shall be in those days.*[165] The Sages dwelt at great lengths on this subject,[166] and it is correct.

When Joshua, the son of Nun, died, may he rest in peace, he transmitted[167] to the Elders all the explanations [of the Torah] that he had received [from Moses], and also all the laws that were inferred in his lifetime, concerning which no argument existed. However, where there was a difference of opinion, the final ruling was in accordance with the view of the majority of the Elders. Concerning them does Scripture state: *And Israel served the Lord all the days of Joshua, and all the days of the Elders who outlived Joshua.*[168] Following this, these Elders taught what they had received from Joshua to the prophets and the prophets taught these laws and their elaborations to one another. No generation went by[169] in which there was no investigation or delving into these matters. The Sages of every generation would consider the teachings[170] of their predecessors as fundamental, and would learn their texts from them, and would generate new ideas. The basic[171] fundamentals were never subject to differences of opinion. The transmission of the Torah teachings proceeded in this manner until the period of the men of the Great Assembly.[172] These were Haggai, Zechariah, Malachi, Daniel, Hananiah, Mishael, Azariah, Ezra the Scribe, Nehemiah the son of Hahaliah, Mordecai, and Zerubabel the son of Sh'altee'el. To these prophets were added Elders from among the craftsmen and smiths[173] and the like to make up the remainder of the 120 [of the Great Assembly]. These, too, deliberated, as did their predecessors, and they proclaimed decrees and enacted ordinations. The last of that Holy[174] group is the first of the Sages mentioned in the Mishnah, namely, Simeon the Righteous, who was the High Priest of that generation.

Time passed until the last of them,[175] Rabbi Judah the Prince our Holy Rabbi, may he rest in peace, who was the outstanding one in his generation, and unique in his time; a man in whom were found all precious attributes and virtuous traits, so much so that he became worthy, in the eyes of the people of his generation, to be called simply our Holy Rabbi [or Rebbe]. His name was Judah. He was the epitome of wisdom and greatness, as they stated: "From the time of Moses our Teacher until Rebbe,[176] we have not seen Torah and greatness in one place."[177] He was unsurpassed in righteousness, humility, and abstinence from wordly pleasures, as they also stated: "When Rebbe died, true humility and fear of sin disappeared."[178] He was also eloquent and more knowledgeable in the Hebrew language[179] than any other man, so much so, that the Sages, of blessed memory, came to learn the explanation of words[180] of Scriptures which were unclear to them[181] from the words of his slaves and servants. This is well-known in the Talmud.[182] He was also endowed with great wealth and property[183] to the point that it was said: "The House Steward of Rebbe was wealthier than King Shapur."[184] Therefore, he was generous with the Sages and with their disciples and he spread Torah in Israel. He collected all the traditions and discussions of the Sages as well as their differences of opinion which had been transmitted [through the generations] from the days of Moses our Teacher until his time. He himself was one of those who received these traditions, since he acquired them from his father Simeon and he from his father Gamliel and he from his father Simeon and he from his father Gamliel and he from his father Simeon and he from his father Hillel who received them from his teachers Shemayah and Abtalion. The latter [received the Torah and its traditions] from Judah the son of Tabbai and Simeon the son of Shetah; they from Joshua the son of Perahyah and Nittai the Arbelite, and they from Jose the son of Joezer and Jose the son of Yohanan, they from Antigonus of Socho, and he from Simeon the Righteous, he from Ezra who was among the last of the men of the Great Assembly, and Ezra from his teacher Barukh the son of Neriah, and Barukh from Jeremiah.[185] Undoubtedly, in a similar manner did Jeremiah receive it from the prophets who preceded him, prophet from prophet, until the Elders who received it from Joshua the son of Nun, and he from Moses.

When he[186] had collected all the views and opinions, he commenced to redact the Mishnah, which incorporates the explanations of all the commandments written in the Torah. Of these, some are teachings received directly from Moses; others are views derived from logical reasoning and concerning which no difference of opinion exists. Others yet are teachings regarding which argumentation occurs between two views; these he included with the debate saying: "This one states thusly, and that one states differently." Even if one Sage is in disagreement with many, the opinion of the one as well as the view of the majority are recorded. This [recording of the opinion of a single person] was done in many discussions to good purpose, as is enumerated in the Mishnah in tractate Eduyot.[187] I will mention these, but only after mentioning a fundamental principle that I see fit to describe here, and that is that a person could ask: "If these explanations of the Torah, as we have enumerated them, were received from Moses, as we have stated in the name of the Sages, that the entire Torah including its generalities, specifics and minutiae were given at Sinai, then what are these special laws that are referred to as Verbal Mosaic Tradition?"[188] The following principle should be understood properly,[189] namely that the explanations received from Moses are without controversy whatsoever because until now we have never found a difference of opinion amongst the Sages at any time from the days of Moses until Rav Ashi, such that one Sage would say, "He who blinds[190] the eye of his friend shall have his eye removed as it is written *An eye for an eye*,"[191] and the other would say, "He is only obligated to pay indemnity (for the blinded eye)." We have also not found any difference of opinion in [the interpretation of] the scriptural verse, *The fruit of splendid trees*,[192] so that one Sage would say it refers to the *etrog*[193] and another would say it refers to quinces or pomegranates or something else. We have further not found a difference of opinion in that the *Avot tree*[194] refers to [anything other than] the myrtle.[195] We have also found no dispute in the interpretation of the verse, *Thou shalt cut off her hand*,[196] that it refers to indemnity; and also not in what Scripture states: *And the daughter of a priest, if she profane herself by becoming a harlot, she profaneth her father; she shall be burnt with fire*,[197] that such a punishment is not implemented unless she is at least bound to a husband.[198] Similarly, regarding the biblical exegesis of a *damsel in whom the tokens of virginity were not found [during the consummation of the marriage]* and who must then be *stoned*,[199] we have not found anyone from Moses until now who disagrees with the one who interprets that this punishment occurs only if she is a married woman and witnesses testify that she committed adultery after betrothal, in the presence of witnesses, after she had been warned. In a similar manner, in all comparable precepts of the Torah, there is no controversy because all their explanations were received from Moses. Regarding these and similar instances did the Sages say: "The entire Torah with its generalities, specifics, and fine details are all from Sinai."[200]

However, although these laws were received through tradition, and no difference of opinion exists concerning them, it is possible for us to derive these explanations from the wisdom of the Torah given to us, through one of the types of deductive reasoning, or through hints in the biblical text,[201] or from allusions or suggestions that may be found in the scriptural text. Thus, one sees the Rabbis in the Talmud theorizing and arguing with one another in the course of a discussion, citing proofs for each of these interpretations and the like, as exemplified by what they stated regarding the scriptural phrase *The fruit of splendid trees*[202]: perhaps these are pomegranates or quinces or the like, until they brought proof for this deduction from the quotation itself[203] "The fruit of a splendid tree" means a tree[204] whose wood[205] and fruit taste equally [good].[206] Another Sage says that this [scriptural phrase] refers to a fruit that dwells in its tree from year to year,[207] [i.e., perennial]. Yet another Sage says it refers to a fruit that always grows near water.[208] All these proofs were not adduced because the matter was unclear to them until they deduced them from one of these proofs. Indeed, we have unquestionably seen from the time of Joshua until the present that it is the *etrog*[209] that is taken with the *lulav*[210] every year and no difference of opinion exists regarding this matter. Rather, the Sages sought out the scriptural hint that pointed to the accepted meaning.

In a similar manner did they deduce their proof regarding the myrtle tree,[211] as well as their teaching that one is obligated to pay financial compensation to one's neighbor whom one has injured in any limb.[212] Similarly, the Sages' teaching concerning a priest's daughter, as in the case mentioned above, indicates that it refers to a married woman.[213] All similar instances follow this fundamental principle.

This is the intent of their statement, "Its generalities and specifics," that is to say matters of law that can be derived through a general proposition, followed by a specifying particular, or through any of the other thirteen principles [through which the Torah may be expounded],[214] were received from Moses from Sinai. Yet, although received from Moses, they are not called Verbal Mosaic Tradition.[215] For we do not say that "the fruit of a splendid tree," meaning the *etrog,* is a Verbal Mosaic Tradition, or that [the law providing that] he who injures his neighbor must pay indemnity is a Verbal Mosaic Tradition, because we accept the general premise that these explanations were all transmitted through Moses, and some have either suggestions in Scripture, or can be derived by some type of deductive reasoning,[216] as we have mentioned. Therefore, only something that has no scriptural allusion nor hint, and that cannot be derived from the Torah by any manner of deductive reasoning, is called Verbal Mosaic Tradition.

For this reason, when we stated that measurements are a Verbal Mosaic Tradition, it was asked of us:[217] Why do you say that these laws are a Verbal Mosaic Tradition? Are not measurements alluded to in Scripture when it states: *A land of wheat and barley (and vines and fig trees and pomegranates, a land of olive oil and honey)?*[218] The answer is that they really are Verbal Mosaic Tradition, and that they do not have any basis for being derived through deductive reasoning. Further, they are not alluded to anywhere in the Torah. Rather they are juxtaposed to this scriptural verse as a device to make them observed and remembered, but they are not of the subject matter of the verse itself.[219] This is the meaning of the rabbinic statement, "The scriptural verse is merely a suggestive support" in the many places where it is found.[220]

I will now list here most of the laws that have been labeled as Verbal Mosaic Tradition. It is possible that these are all those that are extant. Thus, the truth of what I just said will be clarified for you, that not even one of them[221] has been derived through deductive reasoning, nor can any one of them be based upon a scriptural verse, except as merely a suggestive support, as we have just explained. We never find discussions or deductive derivations being sought for them at all, nor were proofs brought for them; rather they were received from Moses, as the Holy One, Blessed be He, commanded him about them.

And these are they: the laws specifying one-half of a *log*[222] of oil to accompany a thanksgiving offering,[223] [the measure of] one-fourth [of a *log*] of oil for a Nazarite[224] offering, and the period of eleven days between two periods of menstruation are Verbal Mosaic Tradition.[225] The rules of extension,[226] solidification,[227] and a bent wall[228] are Verbal Mosaic Tradition.[229] The regulations of measurements,[230] divisions,[231] and partitions[232] are Verbal Mosaic Tradition.[233] The rules of the willowbranch and the water libation are Verbal Mosaic Tradition.[234] The writing of phylacteries on parchment[235] and of a *Mezuzah*[236] on cheaper parchment[237] and of a scroll of the Torah on better parchment[238] are Verbal Mosaic Tradition.[239] The *Shin*[240] of the phylacteries,[241] the knot of the phylacteries, black straps, the foursidedness of phylacteries,[242] and the hollow rim of the capsule of phylacteries[243] are Verbal Mosaic Tradition.[244] The regulation requiring the wrapping of the sections of the phylacteries with their own hair[245] and the sewing of phylactery boxes with their tendons[246] are Verbal Mosaic Tradition.[247] The necessity for writing a scroll of the Torah with ink and on lines[248] is a Verbal Mosaic Tradition. The legal impossibility of sexual intercourse for a girl less than three years of age[249] is a Verbal Mosaic Tradition.[250]

He who sows[251] two kinds of wheat grain in his field and prepares them on one threshing floor is required to give *Pe'ah*[252] once; if on two threshing floors he gives *Pe'ah* twice. This, too, is Verbal Mosaic Tradition.[253]

The fact that garden seeds which are not used as food[254] are considered together [to make up *Kilayim*[255] if they are one twenty-fourth part of what is sown in a Se'ah's space[256] is a Verbal Mosaic Tradition.[257]

The fact that ten saplings scattered over a Se'ah's space permits one to plough the entire Se'ah's space on their account [during the Sabbatical year][258] is a Verbal Mosaic Tradition.[259] The law that if part of a cake of pressed dried figs became defiled one may give a Heave Offering from the clean part therein for the defiled part[260] is a Verbal Mosaic Tradition.[261] *Orlah*[262] everywhere is Verbal Mosaic Tradition.

The *Hazan*[263] may look where the children are reading [but he himself may not read];[264] this is Verbal Mosaic Tradition.[265] The law that a woman who wraps herself in an apron [and attaches an article to it to carry it on the Sabbath], either before her or behind her, [and it became reversed] is culpable[266] is a Verbal Mosaic Tradition.[267] Mixing strong wine into weak wine[268] is permitted by Verbal Mosaic

Tradition.[269] The law that in the lands of Amon and Moab the tithe of the poor is given in the seventh[270] year[271] is Verbal Mosaic Tradition.[272]

Wherever one of these precepts is mentioned in any subsequent part of the Commentary of the Mishnah, there I will explain it in its proper place, with God's help.[273]

As a result, all the laws ordained in the Torah can be classified into five categories, according to the aforementioned principles.

The first category consists of explanations that were received from Moses,[274] which are alluded to in Scriptures, or may be derived by deductive reasoning.[275] Here no difference of opinion exists; rather if someone states, "Thusly I have received it," one should not question it further.[276]

The second category consists of laws that have been called Verbal Mosaic Tradition and no proofs exist for them, as we have mentioned. This, too, is something without controversy.

The third category consists of laws that are derived through methods of deductive reasoning[277] and concerning these disputes occur, as we have mentioned. The final ruling in these cases is according to the opinion of the majority according to the aforementioned principles if the matter can be argued two ways. For this reason, it is stated: "If this is a *halakhah*,[278] we shall accept it for if it is only an inference an objection may be raised."[279] However, differences of opinion and disputes arise only in matters not known to be *halakhah*.[280] Thus we find throughout the Talmud that the Sages delve into the reasons underlying a deductive derivation that is the cause for the argumentation among the disputants, and the Sages state: "What are they arguing about?" or "What is the reason of Rabbi so and so?" or "What is the point of difference between them?" They approach the problem in this manner in some places and clarify the reason that underlies the controversy, as if they say: "Rabbi so and so employs such and such an argument whereas Rabbi so and so relies on such and such an argument," and the like.

However, there are those who think that the laws that are in controversy were also received from Moses, and who further believe that the controversy arose by way of errors in the [traditionally received] *halakhot*, or because of forgetfulness, or because one of the Sages received the correct tradition whereas the other[281] was mistaken in the understanding of what he received, or forgot, or did not understand all that which he was supposed to understand from his teacher. They[282] bring evidence for this contention with the statement, "When the disciples of Shammai and Hillel who had insufficiently served their teachers[283] multiplied, controversy increased in Israel and the Torah became as two Torahs."[284] This type of contention is, by my life, an extremely depraved and base thing and not correct or does not conform to basics. Such a contention blemishes [the reputation of] those people from whom we received the Torah. Such type of reasoning is null and void. That which brought one to believe in this depraved[285] conviction was a paucity of understanding of the words of the Sages that are found in the Talmud because they found the explanation that was received from Moses, and this is correct according to the aforementioned principles, since they did not differentiate between traditionally received fundamentals and the secondary teachings derived by deliberation.

Indeed, if you are in doubt about anything, do not be in doubt concerning the controversy between Bet Shammai and Bet Hillel[286] whether: "After the meal they sweep the floor[287] and then wash their hands"[288] or "They wash their hands and then sweep the floor."[289] Do not think that one of these two views was not received by Moses at Sinai. The reason that is the basis for their argument is that which is mentioned in the Talmud,[290] namely, one of them [Bet Hillel] forbids the use of an unlearned attendant[291] [to remove bread crumbs], whereas the other [Bet Shammai] permits it. The same is true of all similar controversies that are ramifications of this approach.

However, that which the Sages stated, "When the disciples of Shammai and Hillel who had insufficiently served their teachers[292] multiplied, controversy increased in Israel," is a matter that can be simply explained. That is, wherever two people are equal in understanding, in deliberative capacity, and in knowledge of fundamentals [of the Torah] from which to derive their deduced opinions, no controversy at all arises[293] in regard to their reasoning. Should this happen,[294] it will be minute indeed; and thus we do not find a difference of opinion between Shammai and Hillel, save in a few specific *halakhot*. This is because the approaches of both are similar in all that they learn, namely by deductive reasoning. The correct fundamentals with which one is endowed are the same as the fundamentals given to the other. However, when the diligence of their disciples in the study of Torah diminished, and when their power of deductive reasoning weakened, when compared to the reasoning of their teachers Hillel and Shammai, then controversy arose between them during deliberation of many subjects, as each one's opinion was molded by his understanding and the fundamentals with which he was familiar.

In spite of this, one should not condemn them, because we cannot compel two wise men who are discussing a theory to propound it with the understanding of Joshua or Pinchas.[295] We should also not be too critical of what they[296] argue just because they are not as capable as Shammai and Hillel or like one who is greater in knowledge than they.[297] The Holy One, Blessed be He, did not command us to do so;[298] rather, He instructed us to listen to the Sages of our generation as it is stated: *To the judge who shall be in those days.*[299] It is in this manner that controversies arose, and not because they[300] erred in what they heard [from their teachers] and that one is saying the truth and the other nullifies it. How much clearer these matters are to one who delves into them and what a precious principle of our Torah this is!

The fourth category consists of decrees ordained by the prophets and Sages of every generation in order to make a protective fence around the Torah.[301] In a general manner, the Holy One, Blessed be He, commanded us to make such protective laws, and this is what is meant by the statement, *And ye shall keep my charge,*[302] which is traditionally interpreted to mean "Provide protection for my observances."[303] The Sages call these restrictive measures "decrees."[304] Here, too, controversy may arise because one Sage may prohibit something for a specific reason, whereas the other Sage disagrees. This occurs frequently in the Talmud where it is stated that Rabbi so and so decreed such and such because of such and such, whereas Rabbi so and so did not so decree. This, too, is one of the causes of controversies [among Sages in the Talmud].

Thus, for example, the prohibition of eating flesh of fowl with milk is a rabbinical decree to keep one far from transgression. However, the Torah only prohibits milk with flesh of cattle[305] and beasts,[306] whereas the Sages decreed the prohibition of flesh of fowl with milk to keep one far from transgressing an interdiction.[307] There are some who did not agree with this decree, like Rabbi Jose the Galilean who permitted the consumption of flesh of fowl with milk, and all the inhabitants of his town ate this combination, as is well publicized in the Talmud.[308]

Where complete agreement prevails regarding one of the decrees, no one may disobey it in any respect. If a prohibition has been widely accepted throughout Israel, no one should nullify that decree. Even the prophets were not permitted to void it. Thus, it is stated in the Talmud[309] that even Elijah could not abrogate one of the eighteen items that Bet Shammai and Bet Hillel decreed. The reason that is quoted[310] for this is that these prohibitions have spread among all of Israel.

The fifth category consists of laws based on empirical investigation regarding the social behavior of individuals in those matters that do not constitute an addition to or detraction from a biblical commandment[311] or regarding things that are efficacious for people[312] with respect to the observance of the laws[313] of the Torah. These are called "ordinances"[314] and customs. It is prohibited to transgress these in any way since they are accepted by all the people. King Solomon, of blessed memory, has already warned regarding him who transgresses any one of these ordinances[315]: *And whosoever breaketh through a fence will be bitten by a snake.*[316]

These decrees are extremely numerous and are cited in the Talmud and the Mishnah. Some are related to the topic of the forbidden and permitted (foods, marriages, and so forth), and others pertain to civil law.[317] Some of these decrees were ordained by the prophets, such as the decrees of Moses, Joshua, and Ezra, as the Sages have stated: "Moses ordained to the Israelites that they should discuss[318] the laws of Passover in the season of Passover."[319] They further stated: "Moses decreed the benediction 'Who provides,'[320] at the time when the Manna was descending for the Israelites."[321] The decrees of Joshua[322] and Ezra,[323] however, are many [and will, therefore, not be enumerated here]. Yet other decrees [of this social reform type] are attributed to individual Sages as they stated: "Hillel instituted *Pruzbul*";[324] "Rabban Gamliel the Elder decreed";[325] "Rabbi Yohanan ben Zakkai ordained";[326] and often in the Talmud it is stated "Rabbi so and so decreed." Finally, there are some decrees attributed to a multitude of Sages,[327] as they stated: "The Sanhedrin in Usha decreed,"[328] or "The Sages ordained," or "A decree of the Sages." Similar instances are very common.

Thus, all the laws enumerated in the Mishnah can be subdivided into these five categories; some are interpretations received from Moses that are alluded to in Scripture, or can be derived through deductive reasoning;[329] others are Verbal Mosaic Tradition; others yet are laws derived by deductive reasoning but concerning which differences of opinion may arise. Some of these laws are decrees,[330] and others are ordinances.[331]

I will now explain the reason for the recording of both sides of a controversy that arises between two viewpoints. If these legal decisions[332] were written as final rulings[333] as if there were no controversy, and if the opinion of the Sage whose view is not the finally accepted one is omitted, then it is possible that at a later time someone will come along who agreed[334] with the opposing viewpoint, which is the opposite of the one that is recorded as the final ruling. Thus a doubt is raised in our minds, and we might say: How could this person, a trustworthy man, have learned that such and such a thing is prohibited if the Mishnah specifically states that it is permitted, or vice versa? But if all the opinions would be written down for us,[335] this seeming contradiction would be averted. Thus, if anyone would say: "I have heard that such and such is prohibited," we can say to him, "You speak correctly, but it is the view of so and so, and many disagree with him," or "So and so disagrees with him, and the final ruling is according to the dissenting viewpoint," either because his deductive reasoning is more plausible, or because we have found another statement that supports him.[336]

On the other hand, the reason why he[337] recorded the opinion of a single person and that of the majority is that sometimes the final ruling is according to the opinion of the single person and, therefore, he[338] teaches us that if the argument is correct and clear,[339] even if it be that of a single person, it is accepted,[340] though many may argue with him.[341]

The reason for recording the opinion of a single perfect man even though he later withdrew that opinion, such as when the Sages stated, "Bet Shammai say such and such whereas Bet Hillel say such and such, and Bet Hillel reconsidered and taught according to the opinion of Bet Shammai,"[342] is to demonstrate their love for the truth and pursuit of righteousness. For when these great men – righteous, understanding, completely knowledgeable, and of eminent scholarship[343] – saw that the opinions of him who argues with them are more correct than their own and that his[344] deliberations are better, they would change to his viewpoint. All the more so should other people, when seeing the truth in the argument of their opponent, turn to it [and accept it] without being stubborn.[345] This is the meaning of the scriptural phrase *Justice, justice shalt thou follow.*[346] It is concerning this matter that the Sages stated, "Acknowledge the truth,"[347] meaning that even if you could save face[348] with sophisticated counter-arguments, if you know that your opponent's viewpoint is the truth, although your argument may be clearer due to his weakness in expressing himself, or because of your ability in argumentation, withdraw to his viewpoint and abandon the fight.[349]

When the author of the Mishnah considered its editing according to this pattern,[350] he saw fit to divide this work into sections and, therefore, divided it into six sections.

The first section deals with commandments pertaining to the plants of the land, such as laws of prohibited mixtures,[351] laws of the Sabbatical year, *Orlah*,[352] Heave Offerings, Tithes, and other laws of agricultural gifts.[353]

The second section deals with the holidays and the festivals, their requirements and their varying laws,[354] that which is prohibited, desirable and permitted therein, and those laws and commandments that are properly associated with each of these holidays.

The third section deals with conjugal relations

and enumeration of the laws pertaining to relations between men and women, such as the Levirate marriage, *Halitzah*,[355] the marriage settlement document,[356] betrothals and divorces, and all that is deemed necessary to be stated for each of these subsections.

The fourth section deals with civil and criminal laws, disputes between man and his neighbor, trade, business dealings,[357] partnership in real estate, and the like.

The fifth section deals with sacrifices, according to their varying laws and multitude of types.

The sixth section deals with the matter of purifications and their opposites.[358]

Each of these sections is called a Seder.[359] The first section is called Seder Zera'im,[360] the second Seder Mo'ed,[361] the third Seder Nashim,[362] the fourth Seder Nezikin,[363] the fifth Seder Kodashim,[364] and the sixth Seder Tohorot[365] (mnemonic *ZeMaN-NaKaT*).[366]

He[367] began with Seder Zera'im because it deals with laws specifically relating to the plants of the earth,[368] and the plants of the earth represent the sustenance of all living creatures. Since it is not possible for man to survive without consuming food, it would be impossible for him to serve the Lord in any manner. Therefore, he[369] began by speaking of precepts dealing specifically with produce of the land.

Following this, he discusses Seder Mo'ed because this is their sequence in the Torah, as it is stated: *Six years shalt thou sow thy land and shalt gather in the increase thereof; but the seventh year thou shalt let it rest and lie fallow;*[370] and immediately after is stated: *Six days shalt thou do thy work;*[371] and this is followed by: *Three festivals shalt thou celebrate unto me in the year.*[372]

After this he saw fit to have the laws of women precede the laws of damages, in order to follow the Divine approach as in the sequence in Scriptures which states, *if a man sells his daughter to be a maid servant;*[373] *And if men fight and hurt a pregnant woman,*[374] and only then does it state; *if an ox gores a man.*[375] For this reason, he gave Seder Nashim precedence over Seder Nezikin. The Book of Exodus contains these four subjects, that is to say the topics of Seder Zera'im, Seder Mo'ed, Seder Nashim, and Seder Nezikin.

Having described the subject matter of the Book of Exodus, he[376] then moved to the Book of Leviticus, according to their sequence in the Torah. And after Seder Nezikin he established Seder Kodashim and after that Seder Tohorot, because this is their sequence in Scripture. He gave the laws of sacrifices precedence over the laws of defilements and purifications because purifications are first discussed in the portion of Scripture: *And it came to pass on the eighth day.*[377]

After these six categories, which contain all the precepts of the Torah, were collected [to form the Mishnah], he saw fit to subdivide each general category[378] into its topics as appropriate. He called each topic a tractate.[379] Then he further subdivided the subjects within each tractate into parts, and called each part a chapter.[380] After that, he segregated the subjects of each chapter into yet smaller parts so that it is easy to remember them and to teach them. He called each of these smaller parts of a chapter a *halakhah*.[381]

He subdivided the subjects of Seder Zera'im[382] as I will describe. He commenced with tractate Berakhot.[383] The reason for this is that when an experienced physician wishes to maintain the state of health of a healthy individual, he first attends to the diet as the primary therapy. Similarly, this great Sage[384] saw fit to begin [the Mishnah] with Berakhot, since anyone who wishes to eat is not permitted to do so until he has recited a benediction over the food.[385] Therefore, he found it appropriate to begin the Mishnah with tractate Berakhot in order to supply the necessary preparation for partaking of food. So that nothing be lacking in any aspect, he speaks about all the benedictions that a person is obligated to recite both over edibles and for fulfilling other precepts in the Torah. There is no commandment that every person is obligated to fulfill every day except for the recitation of the *Shema*. It would not be correct to speak of the blessings of the *Shema* before speaking of the *Shema* itself, and, therefore, he begins with the words; "From when may one recite the *Shema* . . ."[386] and everything pertaining thereto.

Following this, he returned to the main subject of the order, and that is to speak of the commandments pertaining to the produce of the earth. He began with tractate Pe'ah,[387] which follows Berakhot, because all the offerings[388] that a person is obligated to provide concerning produce are not required until after their cutting.[389] But the obligation of *Pe'ah* exists while the produce is still in the ground, and for this reason he speaks of it first. After Pe'ah he placed tractate Demai,[390] because the poor have a privilege therein, just as they do in *Pe'ah*. So, too, did they[391] state: "One may give Demai produce to the poor for food."[392] After Demai comes tractate Kilayim,[393] because this is their sequence in Scripture in the portion:[394] *Ye shall be Holy,*[395] *Thou shalt not wholly reap the corner of thy field,*[396] and following this is *Thou shalt not sow thy field with two kinds of seed.*[397] He arranged tractate Shevi'it[398] after Kilayim, although it would have been more correct for tractate Orlah[399] to follow Kilayim, because this is their sequence in the Torah,[400] were it not that he knew that *Orlah* is not one of the precepts that a person is compelled to fulfill, since as long as he has not planted any trees there is no obligation of *Orlah*. The Sabbatical year, however, is obligatory for everyone. Furthermore, the Sabbatical year has its own individual section in the Torah[401] and, therefore, he discusses tractate Shevi'it first. He placed tractate Terumah[402] after Shevi'it because the Great Heave Offering is the first gift that one removes from the produce.[403] He placed tractate Maaser Rishon[404] after Terumah because the former follows Terumah in the order of the scriptural text. After Maaser Rishon he placed Maaser Sheni,[405] according to their proper sequence.[406] He placed tractate Hallah[407] next because after one has separated the aforementioned offerings from the produce namely, Heave Offering, First Tithe, and Second Tithe, then one grinds it, makes it into flour and kneads it into dough at which time it becomes subject to the law of *Hallah*. After he completed the discussions regarding grains and its offerings, he began speaking about fruits and thus speaks of *Orlah* after tractate Hallah. After this is tractate Bikkurim[408] because it is in this order that Scripture arranged them: *Orlah* in Leviticus[409] and *Bikkurim* in the portion *When thou shalt come.*[410] He thus completed the subdivision of the subjects in Seder Zera'im[411] into eleven tractates.

He then subdivided Seder Mo'ed[412] into its individual topics,[413] as he did for Seder Zera'im. He began with tractate Shabbat because it is first in importance and because it occurs every seven days and its cycle is most frequent in the time scale.[414] In addition, the portion of Scripture dealing with Festivals[415] begins with the Sabbath.[416] After Shabbat he placed tractate Eruvin[417] because it is of the same subject matter as Shabbat. Following this is tractate Pesahim[418] because it is the first of the commandments given to us by Moses.[419] It is also proximate to the Sabbath in the portion of Scripture dealing with the Festivals.[420] After this he placed tractate Shekalim,[421] according to the sequence in the Torah.[422] And he placed the Day of Atonement[423] after Shekalim, according to their sequence in the Torah, because the precept of Shekalim is in the portion *Ki Tisa,*[424] whereas Atonement is in the scriptural portion *Acharei Mot.*[425] He then completed the subject[426] of the three pilgrimage festivals. Since he had already spoken about Passover above,[427] it remained for him to speak on the subject of Tabernacles,[428] the Festival of Weeks.[429] Concerning the latter, he had nothing to discuss except for those laws that apply to every Festival and those are included in tractate Betzah.[430] He, therefore, placed Sukkah[431] before Betzah because of the multitude of commandments that apply to Sukkot.[432] Of all the portions [dealing with Holy Days] mentioned in the Bible, there remained only Rosh Hashanah[433] and, therefore, after tractate Betzah he speaks about Rosh Hashanah. Thus were completed the discussions about the topics of the Festivals mentioned in the Torah.

He[434] then began to speak of the topics cited by the prophets and these are the days of fasting[435] ordained by the prophets. He, therefore, placed the topic of Fast Days[436] after Rosh Hashanah. After Fast Days he placed Megillah[437] because it is an ordination of the prophets who lived later than those who decreed the fast days.[438] After tractate Megillah, he placed tractate Mo'ed Katan,[439] because there is a connection between it and the time of Purim, in that on both occasions it is forbidden to pronounce eulogies or to fast.[440] Having completed the discussion of various Festivals[441] and their requirements and all that pertains to them, he concluded the subject with tractate Hagigah,[442] which deals with the obligations of the three pilgrimage festivals. He placed it last because its rules are not universally applicable, since the obligation rests only upon males as it is written: And *all thy males shall appear.*[443] Thus, he completed the subdivision of the topics in Seder Mo'ed into twelve tractates.

He then proceeded to subdivide the subject matter of Seder Nashim[444] and commenced with tractate Yevamot.[445] The reason that compelled him to begin with Yevamot and not with tractate Ketubot,[446] since common sense dictates that the latter should more properly precede the former, is because marriage is related to a man's wishes;[447] and the courts do not coerce a man to marry a woman. However, regarding the Levirate marriage,[448] they[449] can do this by telling him:[450] "Either perform *Halitzah*[451] or contract Levirate marriage." It is more appropriate to begin with laws which are compulsory[452] and he[453] therefore commenced with Yevamot and followed it with Ketubot. After Ketubot he lists tractate Nedarim,[454] because the entire scriptural portion dealing with vows speaks of vows of women as it is written: *Between a man and his wife, between a father and his daughter.*[455] When the marriage is completed by the woman coming under the canopy, the husband has the right to void her vows, and for this reason tractate Nedarim is next after Ketubot. After Nedarim he placed tractate Nazir,[456] because Nazirite oaths are also included among the laws of vows and if a woman should make a Nazirite vow the husband can void it and, therefore, he placed Nazir after Nedarim.

Having completed the discussion of matters related to marriage and the laws regarding the voiding of vows, he commenced the topic of divorce because after marriages come divorces,[457] and thus he arranged tractate Gittin[458] after Nazir. And after Gittin is tractate Sotah,[459] because its subject matter is related to the topic of divorce, since if a suspected adulteress is found to have committed adultery one forces both the husband and the wife[460] to go through with divorce proceedings, as I will explain in its proper place.

After Sotah he placed tractate Kiddushin[461] and with it he completed Seder Nashim. One could ask at this point: Why is Kiddushin placed last? It would seem appropriate that it be earlier and listed before Ketubot. You might wish to answer and say that it was not listed before Ketubot in order not to separate Yevamot from Ketubot, since both deal with the same subject, namely, the matter of marriages of women[462] so that their contents be tied together.[463] If so, Kiddushin should have been listed before Gittin in order to follow the logical sequence-first marriage and then divorce. The answer is that the sequence was so arranged because he[464] wished to follow the sequence of the scriptural passage which speaks of divorce before marriage. This is what the Holy One, Blessed be He, stated: *And he shall write her a bill of divorcement and give it in her hand and send her out of his house. And when she is departed out of his house, she may go and become another man's wife.*[465] From the statement *she may become another man's wife* we learn a fundamental teaching of the laws of marriage as is explained in the Talmud:[466] "the process of becoming[467] is compared to the process of departure."[468] And thus the subject matters of Seder Nashim are subdivided into seven tractates.

Following this, he subdivided the subject matter in Seder Nezikin[469] and separated the first tractate thereof into three parts.[470] He began with Bava Kamma,[471] which deals with various agents of injury and how to avoid them, such as an ox, a ditch, consumption,[472] the laws of assault, and their like. A judge is obligated to first litigate the removal of sources of injury from among people.[473] Next follows Bava Metzia,[474] which deals with claims, deposits,[475] hirings, the laws of borrowers and hired laborers, and everything else that is appropriately connected with this topic. This is similar to the sequence in Scripture, namely, after the laws of ox,[476] ditch,[477] consumption,[478] *and if men fight together*,[479] it speaks about the four types of watchmen.[480] Then comes tractate Bava Batra,[481] and its subject matter deals with laws about divisions of property, laws pertaining to dwellings held in partnership, and laws concerning neighbors, and annulment of a sale or transaction due to the discovery of a physical defect therein. It further speaks of the sale and acquisition of property, how to adjudicate these cases, and the laws of bonds[482] and inheritance. This section[483] is described last, because it consists entirely of tradition and legal arguments, none of it being explicit in the Torah.

Having enlightened us concerning the civil laws, he then speaks about the judges who implement these laws and, therefore, placed tractate Sanhedrin[484] after Bava Batra. However, tractate Makkot[485] is attached to tractate Sanhedrin in many ancient texts[486] and is counted as part of it[487] because he[488] speaks of "These are Strangled"[489] and then continues with "These are flogged."[490] This is not a valid reason, however, because it[491] is a separate tractate. It is placed next to Sanhedrin because it is not permissible for anyone save the judges themselves to administer floggings[492] and punishments as it is written in Scripture: *The judge shall cause him to lie down and to be beaten before him according to his wickedness.*[493]

After Makkot he placed tractate Shevu'ot,[494] because the conclusion of the former tractate and the beginning of this latter tractate deal with similar laws and judgments, as is mentioned in the Talmud.[495] Furthermore, it[496] also pertains to the actions of judges in that only a judge can impose an oath.

Having completed the discussion of civil laws and judges and all that pertains to judges' actions exclusively in the matter of corporal punishment,[497] and the imposition of oaths,[498] he[499] then describes the subject of *Eduyot.*[500] Most of the topics in this tractate are the enumeration[501] of all the legal testimonies[502] rendered by trustworthy individuals whose decisions are final rulings.[503] This fact is fundamental for the establishment of laws because testimonies are only to be pronounced before a court. Similarly, all testimony from these people is only pronounced before a court.[504] It is placed after tractate Shevu'ot because

Shevu'ot deals with matters regularly needed throughout the generations,[505] whereas Eduyot are testimonies pronounced before judges at specific times in the past and which were accepted.[506]

Following this he speaks of matters relating to idol worship[507] because its content deals with topics that a judge must know in order to be completely qualified by being familiar with the customs of such idol worship and all that pertains thereto. He will thus know how to pass judgment regarding them. Thus, if one worships Saturn[508] in the manner one worships Venus[509] or if one prays[510] to Jupiter[511] with the prayer usually reserved for Mars,[512] one is not liable to execution, in accordance with the clear tradition.[513] He placed this tractate last because an instance of idol worship happens only very rarely and is an exceptional occurrence.

Having completed the discussion of items necessary for judges, he then began with Avot[514] and did this for two reasons: first, to tell us the truth and the correctness of the oral tradition that was handed down from generation to generation. Therefore, it is proper to revere a most learned Sage[515] and to place him in an honorable position because he bears the tradition. He is to his generation what these earlier Sages were to their generation. Similarly, they said "if we come to investigate the decisions of the Court of Rabban Gamliel [we would be obliged to investigate every court which has existed from the days of Moses until the present]."[516] They further stated that "Samson in his generation is like Aaron[517] in his generation."[518] From this we derive a great moral teaching. People should not say: "Why should we accept the judgment of so and so, or how can we follow the decree of so and so?" But that is not the case, since the judgment does not belong to that particular judge but to the Holy One, Blessed be He, who so commanded us as it is written: *For the judgment is God's.*[519] Indeed, it is all one judgment that was transmitted from one individual to another throughout the generations. The second reason [why tractate Avot follows tractates dealing with laws of judges and judgments] is that he[520] wished to inform us in this tractate the ethical teachings of each of the Sages, may they rest in peace, so that we may learn good traits from them. No one is in greater need of this than judges for if ordinary people would not learn good character, no harm is done to the multitudes, only to those people themselves.[521] However, if a judge is not ethical and modest, he would hurt both himself as well as others with his errors. Therefore, the initial statements in tractate Avot deal with morality for judges as it states: "Be patient[522] in the administration of justice."[523] A judge should conduct himself according to all the ethical preachments included in tractate Avot; he should be patient in rendering justice, and not speedily arrive at a final decision, because if he rushes the possibility arises that there may be dishonesty in that judgment as the Rabbis[524] have stated "a judgment could be dishonest."[525] On the other hand, he should also not unduly prolong a case if he knows well that no dishonesty exists therein, because this is called "suppression of judgment."[526] He[527] should be thorough in the interrogation of witnesses and be careful during this investigation not to say anything that may lead the witnesses[528] or benefit them.[529] He should further not suggest lines of argument for either litigant; this would be called "playing the part of an attorney."[530] He should not degrade himself in the company of common people[531] lest he come to shame,[532] nor should he excessively estrange himself from people lest the needy perish.[533] He should also not seek idleness and pleasures, lest the truth elude him[534] and lusts overcome him. And he should not love authority nor jump to render judgment[535] lest he become suspect. In most of his judgments he should seek compromise. Were it possible for him not to have to render a legal decision all the days of his life but rather arbitrate a settlement[536] between the two litigants, how praiseworthy this would be. If, however, compromise is not possible, he should render a judgment but not force a decision prematurely by setting an arbitrary time limit. Rather he should provide the litigant with sufficient time to plead his case[537] even if his arguments are loquacious and foolish. But if this is not possible, according to what he[538] observes in their[539] arguments,[540] he should render a legal decision immediately. Thus, we have observed the Sages render and execute decisions [without hesitancy, even when it entails punishment, as] with regard to the tying of the hands, the striking by the court officer in administering floggings and punishments, the removal of clothing,[541] the tearing up of authenticated documents if a reason for doing this is found,[542] and many other similar instances. Analogous to these types of action[543] did they state: "Let the law bore through the mountain."[544]

The general rule is that a judge should be like an expert physician who, as long as he can heal by dietary means, does not resort to drugs, but if he sees that the illness is strong and cannot be cured by dietary means [alone], he will then administer mild medications whose action is similar to food such as beverages and preparations that are fragrant and sweet. If he finds the illness is even more serious and the aforementioned items cannot prevail over it nor cure it, he will then employ more powerful drugs to effect healing and give the patient [a purgative medication] to drink such as scammony,[545] mushroom,[546] milk, cactus, and similar medicines that are bitter and distasteful.[547] Similarly, a judge should attempt to arbitrate a compromise; if this is unsuccessful,[548] he should judge with gentleness, humble himself, and speak to the litigants with soft words. If this is unsuccessful because of the truculent nature of one of the disputants who wishes to prevail against the law, he[549] should prevail and strongly rule against him as we have stated.

And it is appropriate that a judge not indulge excessively in worldly pleasures, love of riches, and exalted positions, as stated in Scripture: *Haters of Corruption.*[550] And the Sages further stated [that the scriptural phrase] *The king by justice establisheth the land [but a man who exacteth gifts overthroweth it]*[551] means that if the judge is like a king who is not in need of anything,[552] he *establisheth the land,*[553] but if he is like a priest who moves to and fro among the threshing wheat [collecting his gifts], he *overthroweth* it.[554]

Having thus seen that a judge requires all the foregoing moral teachings in order to conduct himself ethically thereby, it was, therefore, fitting to place tractate Avot after Sanhedrin and those that accompany it[555] because it[556] contains all these ethical principles. To these are added other ethical teachings that lead one to abstention from worldly things, reverence for the Torah[557] and those who study it, the doing of righteousness, and fear of heaven.[558]

Following the presentation of moral principles to judges, he[559] then discusses judicial error, as it is impossible for any human being not to err and transgress. He, therefore, placed tractate Horayot[560] after Avot, and with it completed Seder Nezikin. Thus, he completed the subdivision of the topics in Seder Nezikin into eight tractates.

Following this, he subdivided the order dealing with Holy Things,[561] and began with animal sacrifices,[562] which constitutes tractate Zevahim.[563] After Zevahim comes tractate Menahot,[564] according to their sequence in the Torah.[565] Having completed the topic of Holy sacrifices and what pertains thereto, he speaks of other slaughterings [for ordinary meat consumption], also according to the sequence in Scripture. Thus, after it states, *But in the place which the Lord shall choose in one of thy tribes, there thou shalt offer thy burnt offerings, and there thou shalt do all that I command thee,*[566] it then says, *Notwithstanding thou mayest kill and eat flesh after all the desire of thy soul;*[567] therefore, he placed tractate Hullin[568] after Menahot. After Hullin comes tractate Bekhorot,[569] according to their sequence in Scripture, since after it states, *Notwithstanding, after all the desire of thy soul,* it asserts, *Thou mayest not eat within thy gates the tithe of thy corn, or of thy wine, or of thine oil or the firstlings of thy herd or of thy flock.*[570] After completing the discourse on things whose bodies are Holy,[571] he speaks of money [such as vows of valuation],[572] because these are also Holy and he, therefore, placed tractate Arakhin after Bekhorot. After Arakhin is tractate Temurah,[573] also according to their sequence in Scripture.[574] Having terminated discussions of these topics, he then placed tractate Keritot,[575] within which are enumerated all the offences for which *Karet*[576] is the penalty, and all that is related to that subject. The reason for classifying this topic in Seder Kodashim is that any offense for which the punishment is *Karet* when committed wilfully, if committed unintentionally, the penalty is a sin offering, with few exceptions[577] as will be explained there.[578]

He placed tractate Me'ilah[579] after Keritot because the offenses for which one is obligated to bring a trespass offering are of a lesser severity than those for which a sin offering is required.[580] Tractate Tamid[581] is after Me'ilah, and it is in last place because it does not contain any laws,[582] nor does it concern anything that is forbidden or permitted. Rather, it is only a narrative describing how the daily offering was sacrificed, in order to make it possible to do so forever.[583] After Tamid is tractate Middot,[584] whose content is limited to narratives about the measurements of the Temple, its shape, and the manner of its construction. The benefit to be derived from this is that when the Temple will be rebuilt, one should preserve that shape and that arrangement[585] because that arrangement comes from divine inspiration,[586] as it is stated: *All this [do I give thee] in writing as the Lord hath made me wise by His hand upon me.*[587]

After completing his discussions concerning animal sacrifices and all that pertains thereto, as well as the model of the Temple in which the aforementioned sacrifices are offered, he then juxtaposed to these tractate Kinnim.[588] The entire subject matter of this tractate deals with laws of mixtures of birds, meaning if sacrificial bird offerings became mixed up one with another. This topic is considered last because it is not a necessary occurrence, since they may or may not become mixed up. In addition, all their laws are extremely few, as will be clarified in its place.[589] With this tractate, he completed Seder Kodashim. Thus was completed the subdivision of Seder Kodashim into eleven tractates.

He then subdivided[590] the treatises in Seder Tohorot[591] and began with tractate Keilim.[592] Its subject matter includes the enumeration of all the primary ritual defilements[593] and that which is subject to defilement, as well as that which cannot become defiled so that when we later speak of things that defile we will know which are the things that are susceptible to ritual defilement and which are not. After Keilim comes tractate Oholot,[594] and its subject matter deals with defilements conveyed by a corpse.[595] This tractate is first because it deals with the highest degree of defilement.[596] Following this is tractate Nega'im[597] whose contents deal with the defilement of leprosy because a leper conveys defilement through a common enclosure [tent]. Thus, it is somewhat similar to the defilement of a corpse,[598] as will be explained in its proper place.

After completing discussions of the defilements by a corpse and the like,[599] he began to describe the subject of purification from the aforementioned, namely the red heifer.[600] Thus, after Nega'im he placed tractate Parah.[601] Having concluded the discussion of high degrees of defilement[602] and the manner in which one may become purified therefrom, he speaks of lesser degrees of defilement, which require only the setting of the sun [for purification].[603] He thus placed tractate Tohorot[604] after Parah. It is called *Tohorot*, using euphemistic language,[605] because therein are described the laws of defilement.[606] In addition, knowledge of defilements brings one to knowledge of purification therefrom. If someone would think that the reason for calling the name of the whole order "Seder Tohorot" and the use of the same appellation for one of the tractates thereof *Tohorot* is incorrect, we would answer no, it is not unusual[607] for men of ideas to call a particular item by the name of the general category that includes it.[608]

Having completed the high degrees of defilements and how purification therefrom can be effected, and having spoken about lesser degrees of defilement, he then discusses the laws of cleansings therefrom. He, therefore, placed tractate

Mikva'ot[609] after tractate Tohorot. He placed tractate Niddah[610] last, after all these degrees of defilement, because it is not a general category of defilement that applies to all human beings.[611] He, therefore, placed Niddah after Mikva'ot. It would have been appropriate to have tractate Zavim[612] follow Niddah, but Makhshirin[613] is given precedence over Zavim because Scripture gave it precedence, since the subject of Mackshirin is described in the portion *Vayehi Ba Yom HaShemini,*[614] whereas that of Zavim is not mentioned until the portion of *Metzorah.*[615]

After Zavim he placed tractate Tevul Yom,[616] as it is stated in Scripture: *This shall be the law of him that hath an issue and of him from whom the flow of seed goeth out.*[617] All the aforementioned defilements involve the entire body, meaning that if a person comes in contact with any of them his entire body becomes defiled. And then he began to discuss the defilements of individual limbs by themselves. He, therefore, placed tractate Yadayim[618] after Tevul Yom. After Yadayim is tractate Uktzin.[619] It was set in last place because all its laws are deduced by reasoning, and have no fundamental root in the Torah.

And with this he completed his book.[620] And with this he completed the subdivision of the treatises in Seder Tohorot into twelve tractates. Thus, the sum total of all the tractates of the Mishnah is sixty-one,[621] and the number of chapters is 523.[622]

After this he[623] saw appropriate to mention only the names of Sages closest to him, meaning from Simeon the Righteous and onward.[624] His[625] own words in the Mishnah are extremely concise but contain much information.[626] Everything was clear to him due to the sharpness of his intellect and breadth of his understanding, but to one who is less than he, the subject matter in the Mishnah is difficult to understand,[627] for earlier Sages would only write for themselves.[628] For this reason, one of his pupils, namely, Rabbi Hiyah, saw fit to compose a book following the format of his teacher,[629] to explain the words of his teacher which were not clear. This is the *Tosefta*[630] and his purpose therein is to clarify the Mishnah and to add topics that may be deduced from the Mishnah but only after considerable effort. He[631] discussed these topics to teach us how to interpret and extract knowledge from the Mishnah. So, too, did Rabbi Oshayah.[632]

Rav also redacted the *Beraita*,[633] which is the *Sifra*[634] and *Sifre*.[635] Many others besides these [Sages also compiled commentaries] as they stated:

"When Rabbi so and so came . . . he brought a *Beraita* with him."[636] However, none of these *Beraitot* were as eloquently worded as the Mishnah, nor as logically formulated,[637] nor as concisely worded. Therefore, this work, namely the Mishnah, remains the major compilation and all those other compositions are secondary to it. The Mishnah is the most esteemed work in the eyes of all people. When compared to the other compositions *the daughters saw her and exalted her, Yea the queen and the concubines, and they praised her.*[638] And the goal of all that followed him[639] and that revered group[640] was to understand the words of the Mishnah. Generation after generation did not fail to delve into it and to explain it, each Sage according to his knowledge and understanding. Over the years they differed in the explanation of some of the legal decisions therein.[641] There was no generation of Sages that did not delve into it and reflect upon it and extract new interpretations and learn lessons therefrom, until the time of Ravina and Rav Ashi, who are the last of the Sages of the Talmud.

Rav Ashi retired into solitude to compile the Talmud. He saw fit to do to the words of all those who succeeded our Holy Rabbi as our Holy Rabbi did to the words of all those who followed Moses.

He [Rav Ashi] gathered all the relevant statements and the elucidations of those who studied the Mishnah and the explanations of the commentators, and he clarified the traditional teachings and assembled them. He mastered all this with his knowledge and broad spirit and love of learning with which the Holy One, Blessed be He, endowed him, and he compiled the Talmud.

His intention therewith consisted of four things: The first is to clarify the Mishnah and all the various interpretations given to explain the expressions used in the Mishnah about which there is no final decision, and the point of view of each commentator who contends with his colleague, and the revelation of the correct point of view.[642] This was his primary goal.[643] The second goal was to provide the final decision in a legal matter according to the view of one of the two discussants who differ in the Mishnah or in its interpretation, or in that which should be learned therefrom or that which can be compared to the Mishnah. The third goal [of Rav Ashi in redacting the Talmud] concerns the novel interpretations of matters that the Sages of each generation extracted from the Mishnah and the elucidation of the general principles and proofs that they learned therefrom. They based their decisions upon[644] the *Tanna'im* who make statements in the Mishnah, until all that which could be elicited[645] therefrom was done, as well as the decrees and ordinances that were proclaimed from the time of Rebbe until his time.[646] The fourth goal concerns homiletical expositions that are appropriate according to the content of each chapter in which such an exposition is found.

This fourth goal, that is to say homiletical expositions as found in the Talmud, should not be considered as being of small virtue or of little value. Rather, it has an extremely important purpose in that it is composed of profound allusions and marvelous topics. If one would profoundly scrutinize these homiletical expositions, one would appreciate their incomparable excellence. These expositions reveal divine matters, as well as fundamental verities that learned Sages concealed [and did not wish to disclose], and which philosophers spent generations [trying to understand]. If you will look into these homiletical expositions, according to their simple sense, you will find therein things that are exceedingly difficult to comprehend.[647]

The Sages intentionally did this to wondrous matters.[648] One reason is to sharpen the understanding of those who study, but also to blind the eyes of the foolish whose hearts will never be enlightened. Were one to expose the truth before them, they would turn away therefrom, according to the lack in their nature, as it is written concerning them and their kind: "One does not reveal the secret to them, since their intellect is not adequate to receive the truth in its purity."[649]

Some of the Sages even kept the mysteries[650] of the Torah from each other. They related[651] that a man from amongst the Sages happened to meet individuals who were experts in the "Work of Creation"[652] while he was an expert in the "Work of the Chariot."[653] He said to them: Teach me the "Work of Creation" and I will instruct you in the "Work of the Chariot." They replied: So be it. After they had instructed him in the "Work of Creation," he refused to teach them the "Work of the Chariot." Heaven forbid that he did this out of jealousy or because he wished to be superior to them! Such traits are despicable even for the lowliest person; how much more so for great people. Rather, he did this because he saw that he was prepared to receive what they had to offer[654] but he did not find them suitable to receive the knowledge that he possessed. He supported the correctness of his view in this matter with the statement of Solomon:[655] *Honey and milk are under thy tongue.*[656] The Sages, of blessed memory, interpreted this phrase and stated that the explanation of these words is that the sweet concepts with which the soul delights are comparable to the delight of the sense of taste with honey and milk and should not be spoken nor come out from under the tongue under any circumstances. This is the meaning of the phrase *under thy tongue*; that is, these matters are not of those which are suitable to teach[657] and should not be expounded upon in public. Rather, one alludes to them with hidden allusions in various books. And if the Holy One, Blessed be He, removes the veil from the heart of the one whom He desires, the one who has toiled[658] in their[659] study, such a person will understand them according to the strength of his intellect. Regarding the study of Torah and one's endeavors therein, it is for a person but to direct his heart to the Lord and to pray before Him, and to supplicate that He impart understanding to him and help him and reveal to him the mysteries hidden in the Holy Scriptures. Such do we find by King David, of blessed memory, who did so when he said: *Open Thou mine eyes, that I may behold wondrous things out of Thy law.*[660]

And when the Holy One, Blessed be He, reveals hidden secrets of the Torah to a person, he should conceal that which was revealed to him, as we have mentioned. And if he makes a slight allusion thereto, he should only present this allusion to one whose intellect is complete and whose righteousness is well known, as is explained and clarified in numerous instances in the Talmud. Therefore, it is not proper for a complete man to divulge what he knows of these mysteries, save to one who is greater than he or equal to him. For if he reveals this knowledge to a fool, although the latter may not sneer at it before him, it will not find favor in his eyes.[661] Therefore, the wise man states: *Speak not in the ears of a fool, for he will despise the wisdom of the words.*[662] Furthermore, one should only teach in public by way of epigram and parable, so as to include women and young children so that when their intellect fully matures, they will understand the meanings of those parables. To this matter did King Solomon allude, when he stated: *To understand a proverb and a metaphor; the words of the wise and their epigrams.*[663]

It is for this reason that the Sages, of blessed memory, speak with allusions in divine matters. Therefore, if a person encounters one of their sayings that seems to contradict common sense according to his understanding, he should not consider the failure to understand these matters as a defect of the matters themselves; rather one should attribute the failure to inadequacy of one's intellect. And if one encounters one of their homilies, which is very difficult to understand even in its literal [or simple] meaning, one should be greatly grieved that one's intellect cannot comprehend the matter, so that all truths become extremely distant [from one's understanding]. For the intellects of different people differ just as their temperaments[664] differ; just as the temperament of one person is good and closer to the mean than the temperament of another person, so too the intellect of one person is more correct and complete than the intellect of another person. And there is no doubt that the intellect of one who understands an important matter is not like the intellect of one who does not understand that matter. The former possesses "actual intellect" and the latter only "potential intellect." Therefore, there are things that to certain people are extremely correct and clear, but to others are remote and unattainable according to their level of wisdom.

And I will give you a simple example. Let us ask a man proficient in the sciences of medicine, arithmetic, and music, expert in the laws of nature, clear thinking and intelligent, but totally lacking knowledge in the science of geometry and in the science of astronomy: What do you think of a person who claims that the body of the sun, which we perceive as a small circle and which is a spherical body, that the size of that sphere[665] is one hundred sixty-six and three-eighths times the size of the earth's sphere, and that the earth's sphere, in terms of whose measurements we calculated the sun's measurements, is a globe whose circumference encompasses twenty-four thousand miles,[666] and in this way one can derive the knowledge of how many miles there are in the refraction of the sun's sphere? There is no doubt that the above clear thinker who is knowledgeable in all the sciences that we have enumerated[667] will not find it possible to accept the validity of this claim and he would find it untenable.[668] At first thought, his common sense would dictate that this claim is absurd.[669] For how can man who stands on one handbreadth of earth know the dimensions of its framework and its circumference and its surface measurements as well as he knows the measurement of one piece of land? And in regard to the sun, which is in the heavens extremely distant from him and even its clear observation is not possible since only its rays can be perceived, how can this man reach upward to measure it and be precise in its dimension to a fraction of three-eighths? This is an absolute absurdity. There is no doubt in his mind that this claim should be avoided.

However, if he becomes familiar with books of geometry and studies appropriately the topics that pertain to the structure of spheres and other matters relating to geometrical forms and then proceeds to the book on this subject,[670] or the like – that is, the astronomical book known as the book *Al-Magesti*[671] – then this matter [regarding the dimensions of the sun] will become elucidated to him and the matter will be clear to him and unquestionable because it was already verified through a sign. And he will no longer distinguish between the truth that the sun has these dimensions[672] and the fact that the sun exists.[673] And he will accustom his intellect to fully believe in the truth of this matter that at first is extremely hard for him to accept, and he will have full confidence therein. All this can occur on the assumption that the man to whom we posed our question is a man who is knowledgeable in other sciences[674] and has a clear mind and rapidly understands. The question that we asked is one of the learned questions,[675] which is one of the levels from which one can ascend to divine matters.[676]

How much more difficult is the situation of one

who has not studied at all[677] and is not prepared at all in any manner but proceeded directly from his mother's lap to his wife's lap.[678] If we were to ask him any of the divine questions that require homiletical expositions, there is no doubt that these would be as remote from his comprehension as the heaven is distant from the earth, and his intellect would be too minuscule to comprehend any one of them.

Therefore, we should establish their truth in our hearts and deliberate well on them and not be hasty in rejecting any one of them; rather if any part of one of them is far from comprehension in our eyes, let us become proficient[679] in the sciences until we understand their meanings in that matter, if our intellect can at all comprehend that important matter. For although the Sages[680] were diligent in their learning and sought understanding and preparedness, and associated themselves with greatness and avoided worldly pleasures,[681] yet they would attribute a lack of comprehension to themselves, when they compared themselves to those that preceded them. And this is what they [meant when they] stated:[682] "The hearts[683] of the ancients are like the door of the *Ulam*,[684] but those of the latter generations are not even[685] like the eye of a fine needle." How much more so does this apply to us, we from whom wisdom and knowledge has been lost as the Holy One, Blessed be He, told us: *Therefore, behold, I will again do a marvelous work among this people, even a marvelous work and a wonder; and the wisdom of their wise men shall perish, and the prudence of their prudent men shall be hidden.*[686] This scriptural phrase has characterized each one of us with four things: weakness of intellect, strong lusts, laziness in the quest for wisdom, and diligence in the pursuit of worldly matters, the "four bad judgments."[687] How can we not but attribute this lack [of knowledge and understanding] to ourselves when we compare ourselves to them?[688]

Because the Sages know this matter and all their words are lucid and pure without imperfections, we are commanded and warned not to deride them. And they stated: "He who mocks at the words of the Sages is punished with boiling excrement,"[689] and there is no greater boiling hot excrement than foolishness that leads to mockery. Therefore, the only person who is ever found to deride their words is one who seeks lust and attributes value to sensual pleasures and whose heart is not bright with any illuminating light.

Because of their knowledge and the truth of their words they filled their lives with [the study of Torah] and commanded us to be zealous in this regard during the night[690] and at the ends of the day[691] and they made it[692] the ultimate, and it is really so. And they also stated: "The Holy One, Blessed be He, has nothing in this world save the four cubits of *halakhah*."[693] One should delve discerningly into this matter because, if one understands it superficially, one would consider it to be far from the truth, as if the four cubits of *halakhah* alone represent the ultimate and the other sciences and wisdoms are secondary. And during the time of Shem and Eber and after them when there was no *halakhah*,[694] can we then say that the Holy One, Blessed be He, had no part in the world at all? But if one delves discerningly and deeply into this matter, one observes therein wondrous wisdom and one finds that it comprises many eternal truths. I will explain this for you so that it may serve as an example for you in all other matters that you come across. Therefore, pay close attention thereto.

The ancients[695] made a profound investigation according to their understanding and the strength of their intellect, until it was firmly established in their minds that everything that exists must of necessity have a purpose for which it was created, because not a thing exists for naught. When this general principle became confirmed in their minds, they began to categorize all existing things to know the purpose for each species. They saw that every artificially created object has a known purpose and one need not investigate it. For a craftsman does not create an object until its purpose is clearly depicted in his mind. For example, the blacksmith does not make a saw until he contemplates how he can split these woods, which are fused together. He then pictures the shape of a saw in his mind and begins to make it in order to cut therewith. Thus, the purpose of the saw is to cut therewith. Similarly, the purpose of a spade is to dig therewith, and the purpose of a needle is to sew one garment to another, and similarly for all things whose existence is due to artificial construction.[696]

However, regarding those things whose existence is due to divine workmanship and the wisdom of nature, such as various types of fruits and grasses and metals and stones and animals — the purpose of some can be understood with very little study, whereas the purpose of others cannot be understood except after intensive investigation. The purpose of yet others is so obscure and hidden that it is not understood at all unless it were made known through a vision or through the power of prognostication. But it is not possible to know their purpose through scientific investigation because it is not within the power of man to investigate and to understand why there exist in nature some ants with wings and some without wings; and why there exist worms with many legs and others with fewer legs; or what is the purpose of this worm or that ant. However, regarding things that are larger than these, and whose function is more obvious—there are differences of opinion among scientists as to the purpose of their creation. The more learned and more diligent the scientist whose understanding is lucid, the more he knows that purpose.

Therefore, when the Holy One, Blessed be He, gave to Solomon the wisdom He promised him,[697] he understood the purposes of [the creation of] the aforementioned as much as is possible for a person to understand since he is only human. And Solomon speaks of the purpose of trees and grasses and varieties of living creatures, as written in Scripture: *And he spoke of trees, from the Cedar that is in Lebanon even unto the hyssop that springeth out of the wall; he spoke also of beasts and of fowl and of creeping things and of fishes.*[698] This is an indication that indeed the Divine Spirit was in him. And later it is stated: *And there came of all peoples to hear the wisdom of Solomon.*[699]

However, in general, all things that exist under the lunar sphere exist for man alone. Of all the types of animals, some were created to feed him, such as sheep and cattle and the like, and others that have a different benefit such as the donkey to transport for man that which he cannot carry by hand, and horses to traverse a great distance in a short time. There are yet other types [of animals] whose purpose is not known to us; yet they benefit man though he does not recognize it. Similarly, among fruits, some are to feed man, and some are to heal his sicknesses. The same applies to grasses and so, too, to all other types of creation.

If we find living creatures and plants that have no apparent function and do not serve as food according to our understanding, it is due to a limitation of our understanding. Of necessity, every grass and every fruit and every type of living being, from the elephant to the worm, has some usefulness for man. Proof for this is the fact that in every generation benefits of grasses and various fruits that were not apparent to our predecessors become revealed and many benefits are derived therefrom. It is not within the ability of man to completely encompass in his mind the values of all the plants of the earth but their purposes become revealed through the generations by experience.

And if one would ask: why were fatal poisons such as the herb called "bayish"[700] and "blood grass"[701] created if man perishes by them and they are of no value to him? Know that they do have benefits for although one may die by ingesting them, one does not die if one applies them [as a compress] on the outside of the body. If one recognizes that man derives great benefit from different types of vipers,[702] all the more so [does man benefit] from those things that are less harmful.

Now when we realize that the purpose of all these creations is for the existence of man, we are obliged to also investigate why man exists, and what is his purpose. If one delves deeply into this matter, one finds that man has many activities. All varieties of living beings and trees have only a single activity or, perhaps, two activities but a single purpose as we observe that the date-palm has the sole activity of producing dates. The same applies to other trees. Similarly, among animals some such as the spider only weave and some such as the swallow[703] only build and others such as the ant hoard.[704] However, a man can perform many different tasks and, therefore, each of his activities has been scrutinized, one by one, to know which of these activities was the main purpose in man's creation. And it was found that only one activity is his purpose in life and all his other activities are only to insure the fulfillment of that cardinal activity, which is the attainment of intellect and the proper understanding of the fundamental truths.[705]

For it is not logical that man's major purpose is to eat or to drink or to engage in copulation or to build a house or to be a king[706] because these are all passing occurrences and do not add to his essence.[707] Moreover, he shares all these activities[708] with other types of living creatures. Wisdom, however, is that which is added to his essence and moves him from status to status, from a lower status to a higher status, because he was first only a potential person [in essence] and then became an actual person. For man, before he acquires knowledge, is no better than an animal for he is not different from other types of animals except in his reason. He is a rational living being. The word *rational* means the attainment of rational concepts.[709] The greatest of these rational concepts is the understanding of the Oneness of the Creator, Blessed and Praised be He, and all that pertains to that divine matter.[710] All other sciences[711] serve only to prepare one toward the attainment of divine knowledge. A complete discussion of this matter would be extremely lengthy.

However, concomitant with the attainment of intellect, man is obligated to abandon excessive indulgence in physical pleasures, because the beginning of intelligence is to comprehend that the soul is destroyed from the building of the body and the building of the body is at the expense of the destruction of the soul. For when man chases after lusts and gives in to his sensual desires and loses his intellect to his lusts, so that he is no different than animals and ostriches[712] who conceive only of eating, drinking, and copulation, then the divine capacity, that is intelligence, will not be recognized in him and he will be as isolated primeval matter sinking in the primeval sea.[713]

It seems clear from all these introductory remarks that the purpose of this world, and all that is contained therein, is [to help make] a wise and good-natured man.[714] If a person of the human race acquires knowledge[715] and deeds, a man in this category is the ultimate goal for whom the world was created. Knowledge means the perception of truths and the attainment of all knowledge that it is possible for a man to attain. Deeds refer to normal conduct and action in regard to natural matters;[716] one should not be immersed in them nor partake of them, save that which is required to maintain one's body and to improve one's personal characteristics.[717]

This matter is not only known from the prophets but Sages of ancient peoples who never saw the prophets nor heard their words were already aware that man is not perfect unless there is contained in him intelligence and good deeds. Suffice the words of the most renowned philosopher[718] who said: "God's goal for man is that he be discerning and righteous."[719] For if man is wise and discerning, but chases after his lusts, he is not truly wise, for the beginning of wisdom dictates that man not partake of physical delights, save for the maintenance of his body. And in our commentary upon tractate Avot we will complete the discussion on this matter and elucidate it properly.[720]

Similarly, we find that the prophet rebukes one who claims that he is wise at a time when he transgresses against the laws of the Torah and chases after his lusts. This is what is meant by:[721] *How do you say "we are wise and the law of the Lord is with us"?*[722] Conversely, if a person is God-fearing and self-denying and distances himself from worldly delights – save those required for the maintenance of his body – and follows the correct[723] path in all matters of nature and maintains all good traits, but is not learned, this person is also lacking in perfection, but he is more complete than the former,[724] because his deeds are not performed because of a clear understanding and fundamental recognition [of the reason therefor].[725] Therefore, the Sages, of blessed memory, said: "A boorish person cannot be a sin-fearing man, nor can an ignorant person be truly pious"[726] as we have explained.

And whoever says that an ignorant person is pious contradicts the Sages who made the aforementioned definitive statement. He also contradicts common sense.[727] Therefore, we find throughout the Talmud the commandment: *that you may learn them* and afterward *to perform them.*[728] Learning is mentioned before performance because, through understanding, man will come to action but through performance man does not attain understanding. This is what the Sages meant when they said: "Study leads to action."[729]

There now remains one question and that is the following: You have been told that there is nothing purposeless in divine wisdom and that among all the created beings below the lunar sphere man is the most important, and the purpose of the human species is the attainment of intelligence.[730] If so, why did God create all those people who do not reach wisdom? We observe that most people are completely devoid of knowledge and only pursue their lusts, and the learned man who is self-denying is rare and unusual; there is found only one in each generation.

The answer is that all those unlearned people were created for two reasons. One, to serve that unique individual, for if all people were learned and philosophical the world would be destroyed and all human beings would perish from the world in a short time since man lacks much and has many needs. He would then have to learn ploughing and harvesting and threshing and grinding and cooking and the making of utensils for all these tasks, in order to attain his alimentary needs. Similarly, he would have to learn spinning and weaving to weave his clothing. [He would also have] to learn to build in order to construct himself a place of shelter, and to manufacture tools for all these labors. Not even the lifetime of a Methusaleh[731] would suffice to learn all these tasks that a person of necessity requires for his maintenance. If so, when would such a person learn and study to understand through wisdom? Therefore, all those people were created to perform these acts that the world needs, whereas the learned person was created for himself.[732] Thus is the world built and wisdom found therein.

How beautiful is the proverb that states: "Were it not for fools, the world would be desolate." For there is no greater folly than a man who has a feeble soul and a weak physical constitution who travels from the beginning of the second region of the seven inhabitable districts until the end of the sixth[733] and who traverses oceans in the winter and through deserts during extreme heat in the summer and endangers himself by exposure to different types of wild animals in order to possibly earn a *dinar*. And when he assembles some of those *dinars* for which he gave his entire soul,[734] he commences to distribute them to laborers to build for him a permanent foundation on virgin ground with lime and stones, in order to construct an edifice to last for hundreds of years. Yet he clearly knows that there do not remain in his lifetime enough years to even survive a structure made of reeds. Is there a greater folly than this? So, too, all the delights in the world and physical lusts and folly are essential for the building of the world. Therefore, the Sages, of blessed memory, called an unlearned person *Am HaAretz*,[735] that is to say they were created only to build the earth and, therefore, they[736] associated their[737] name with the earth.

And if a man say: "Behold, we observe a foolish and stupid man who lives in tranquillity in the world without toiling therein. Others serve him and conduct his business dealings for him. And sometimes the one who conducts his business is a learned man." The matter is not as this man perceives it because the reason for the tranquillity of that foolish man is so that he, in turn, serves a man whom the Creator wishes him to serve. Though while he is satisfied with his great wealth and position,[738] he instructs his servants to build a gigantic palace or to plant a large vineyard just as kings and the like do. This palace will be ready for the righteous man who might come in later days and one day seek refuge in the shade of one of the walls of that palace, and this refuge saves him from death. There may be taken one day from that vineyard a little wine to make theriac therewith to save a perfect man who was bitten by a viper.[739] Such is the conduct of the Holy One, Blessed and Exalted be He, and His wisdom, by which He endowed nature [to fulfill] *counsels of old, in faithfulness and truth.*[740] This matter was expounded by our Sages who stated:[741] "Ben Zoma was once sitting on the Temple Mount and saw a crowd of Israelite festival pilgrims. And he said: 'Blessed is He who has created all these to serve me,' "[742] for he was unique in his generation.

The second reason for the existence of people

who have no wisdom pertains to the fact that wise people are extremely few, for thus was it decreed by Divine Wisdom. One may not ask, "Why was this decreed," in regard to the matter of the first wisdom [of creation] just as one may not ask, "Why are there nine spheres[743] and seven planets and four essential elements?"[744] For all these and all their like were decreed from the beginning of creation. You can see that the Sages, of blessed memory, explained this matter in the statement of Rabbi Simeon beu Yohai regarding those of his generation:

"I have seen people of merit[745] and they are but few. [If there be a thousand, I and my son are among them; if a hundred, I and my son are among them]; and if only two, they are I and my son."[746] Therefore, the masses were created to provide company for the meritorious.

Lest you consider this benefit to be of small value, on the contrary, it is more significant than the first.[747] For one sees that the Holy One, Blessed be He, left the wicked in the land of Israel to provide company for the righteous. This is the meaning of the scriptural verse *I will not drive them out from before thee in one year lest the land become desolate.*[748] This subject was also explained by the Sages who said: "What is meant by *For this is the whole*

INTRODUCTION TO MISHNAH COMMENTARY

man[749] . . . the whole world was created only as a companion for him?"[750] means to be a companion for him.

It is thus clear from all that we have said that the purpose of everything that exists in the present imperfect world[751] is to serve the perfect man who is composed of wisdom and good deeds, as we have explained. And since we learn these two things, namely wisdom and good deeds, from the explicit or only alluded-to teachings of the Sages we know the correctness of their statement that "the Holy One, Blessed be He, in His world has only the four cubits of *halakhah*."[752]

We have digressed considerably from the subject matter with which we were concerned. However, we have discussed matters that strengthen one's faith and stimulate the quest for learning. They are not easily assessed, in my opinion. And I will now return to my original subject matter.

When Rav Ashi completed the redaction of the Talmud as we know it today, the beauty of its arrangement and the immensity of its value testify about him that: *He is one in whom is the spirit of the Holy God.*[753] Within Rav Ashi's redaction of the Talmud,[754] there are to be found thirty-five tractates. There is no [Talmud, i.e, Gemara] at all in Seder Zera'im,[755] except for tractate Berakhot alone, and none for tractate Shekalim in Seder Mo'ed,[756] and none for tractate Eduyot nor for tractate Avot in Seder Nezikin,[757] and none for tractate Middot and tractate Kinnim in Seder Kodashim.[758] And we do not find any [Gemara] in Seder Tohorot,[759] except for tractate Niddah alone. And afterward Rav Ashi died in Babylon after he completed the Talmud, as we have described.

The Sages of the land of Israel did the same, that is to say that which Rav Ashi did [in Babylon], and they composed the Jerusalem Talmud.[760] Its editor is Rabbi Yohanan. There are five complete Orders in the Jerusalem Talmud, but Seder Tohorot has no Talmud [i.e., Gemara] at all, neither in the Babylonian nor Jerusalem except for tractate Niddah alone, as we have mentioned. But a person can interpret this latter Order after much toil and great effort and he might be aided by the *Tosefta*[761] and *Beraitot*,[762] and collections of laws assembled from the entire Talmud that pertain to the subject matter [in Seder Tohorot]. And one can extract the general principles of the tractates [in Seder Tohorot] and their ramifications from those aforementioned laws, as you will see in our commentary on that Order[763] with God's help.

And when all the Sages died, may their memory

be blessed, the last of them being Ravina and Rav Ashi,[764] the Talmud was already completed. The intent of anyone that followed them was only to comprehend the words that they composed for there is naught that one can add to or delete therefrom.[765] Therefore, the *Geonim*[766] composed their many commentaries but, according to the best of our knowledge, not one of them succeeded in completing a commentary on the entire Talmud. Some were limited by the brevity of their years and others were impeded by preoccupation with legal judgment concerning the affairs of people. They nevertheless composed works of legal decisions,[767] some in Arabic and others in Hebrew such as the *Halakhot Gedolot,*[768] the *Halakhot Ketuot,*[769] the *Halakhot Pesukot,*[770] the *Halakhot of Rav Acha of Shabcha,*[771] and others. The legal decision coded by the great teacher Rabbi Isaac, of blessed memory,[772] suffices to supplant all the others, because the [code of Alfasi] includes all the legal judgments and decisions needed in our times, that is to say, the time of Exile.[773] He clarified and corrected all the errors that crept into legal works that antedated him. We cannot find difficulty therein save in very few legal decisions, certainly less than ten.[774] But the extant works of all the *Geonim* are as varied as the *Geonim* are themselves but an understanding person who is an expert in the Talmud can recognize the quality of each *Gaon* from the latter's statements and commentaries.

And when the generations passed until our time,[775] we conducted ourselves as did our predecessors to investigate and to expound and to be diligent, according to our capabilities, to attain that which we believe is for our benefit before God.[776] And I have assembled all that has come to my hand from the commentaries of my father,[777] of blessed memory, and others besides him in the name of Rabbi Joseph HaLevi.[778] I swear[779] that the understanding of the Talmud by that man is astounding to anyone who delves into his statements and the depth of his deliberations to the point that I can say of his line of thought: *And equal unto him there was no king before him.*[780] I have also collected all the legal decisions that I found in his commentaries,[781] in addition to those commentaries that originated with me, according to the weakness of my intellect, and those that I reached through learning. And I composed a commentary on three Orders of the Mishnah; Mo'ed, Nashim, and Nezikin, with the exception of four tractates concerning which I am presently endeavoring to write a bit but have not yet found spare time to do so. I have also written a commentary on tractate

Hullin[782] because of the great need therefor. This is the great task in which I have been engaged, together with the learning that I have been acquiring.

Following this, I saw proper to compose a commentary on the entire Mishnah, for which there is a great need as I will elucidate at the end of this introduction. That which led me to compose this work is the fact that I saw that the Talmud does for the Mishnah that which would never have been possible for anyone to arrive at[783] by his own reasoning. Thus, the Talmud discusses certain principles, and states that a given Mishnah refers to a particular aspect of a subject, or that a certain Mishnah lacks certain words and the text should properly be read thusly, or that such and such a Mishnah is so and so's statement and his viewpoint is such and such. Furthermore, the Talmud adds to the words of the Mishnah and deletes from them.

And I felt that if this composition would encompass the entire Mishnah, according to the intent that I will explain, four great benefits would derive therefrom: The first is that we present the correct interpretation of the Mishnah and the explanation of its words for if you were to ask the greatest of *Geonim* for the explanation of a *halakhah* from a

Mishnah, he would not be able to answer at all, unless he were to remember by heart the talmudic discussion regarding that *halakhah,* or he would say: I will search for what is said on this matter in the Talmud, and it is not possible for any person to remember the entire Talmud by heart. It is particularly difficult when a single legal decision of the Mishnah is expounded upon over four or five pages of Gemara since talmudic discussions move from topic to topic [within the same overall theme] with arguments and questions and resolutions to such an extent that only a person who is an expert in talmudic deliberation can extract the essence of the discussion of the explanation of that Mishnah. And this confusion would be compounded if the *halakhah* in the Mishnah is one of those whose explanation is not completely presented in one place but in two or three tractates.

The second [value of my Mishnah Commentary] consists of the final legal decisions that I clearly enunicate next to the explanation of each *halakhah* according to the opinion of the Sage whose viewpoint is accepted as final.

The third [benefit of my Mishnah Commentary] is to serve as an introduction for anyone beginning to delve into talmudic study. He can learn therefrom an approach to investigating statements and their explanations. He will then be as one who has encompassed the whole Talmud and it will greatly help him throughout the Talmud.[784]

The fourth benefit is to serve as a reminder for one who has already learned and is knowledgeable, so that all that he learned remains before him and his learning and studying is orderly in his mouth.[785]

And when I depicted these matters for myself, I strengthened myself to write this composition that I prepared. My intent in this work is to explain the Mishnah as it is explained in the Talmud and to cite only the correct explanations and to eliminate those explanations that are refuted in the Talmud. And I will state the reasons why the matter was decided in that way and the reasons why differences of opinion arose between discussants in some arguments, and according to which viewpoint the final decision is accepted as explained in the Talmud. And I will be careful in all this to be concise, so that the reader will not be left with any doubt because this work[786] is not meant to provide understanding to rocks,[787] but to instruct those who can comprehend.

And I saw proper that my composition should be arranged according to the custom of all the commentators, that is to say I will quote the text of the Mishnah until the end of the legal decision and will then discuss the explanation of that legal decision as we have specified. After this, I will quote the next legal decision and [discuss its explanation] and so on until the end of that Mishnah. And any legal decision that is self-explanatory I will simply cite without discussing it.

And I know that every place where the school of Shammai differ in opinion from the school of Hillel, the final legal decision is according to the view of the school of Hillel, except in the known instances where the final decision is in accordance with the view of the school of Shammai.[788] In only those instances, when I will explain them, will I state that the final decision is in accord with the school of Shammai.

Similarly, in every anonymously quoted Mishnah in which there is no difference of opinion, the final decision is as it is stated in the Mishnah[789] except in a very rare instance.[790] In those unusual cases, I will specifically state that this anonymous *halakhah* is refuted and does not represent the final legal decision. For the remaining differences of opinion, I will not require you to engage in much thought;[791] rather, I will immediately state according to whom the final decision is. Even if there is an individual against a majority, I will state that the final decision is in accord with the majority.[792] May the Lord guide us in the path of truth and aid us to avoid the opposite,[793] with His help, may He be Exalted.

And I saw proper to cite ten chapters before I commence my commentary but these, as I have faith in God, have no great significance in regard to our subject.[794] However, it is good for anyone who wishes [his knowledge of] the Mishnah to be complete to know them.

The first chapter lists Sages[795] mentioned in the Mishnah in whose names traditions are stated. The second chapter lists Sages mentioned in the Mishnah because of an occurrence that once happened to them or because of some moral teaching that they taught or because of a homiletical exposition that they expounded. The third chapter regards knowledge we have concerning the ancestry of the Sages of the Mishnah. The fourth chapter lists the Sages who lived in each generation. The fifth chapter describes, as far as is known, who among them is the disciple and who is the teacher. The sixth chapter seeks to reveal unidentified names[796] and to aid in their identification.[797] The seventh chapter mentions their seniority, according to the author [of the Mishnah, Rebbe]. The eighth chapter associates [various Sages with] certain countries, persons, and families. The ninth chapter lists those Sages among whom differences of opinion were prevalent in most of their discussions. The tenth chapter deals with the multitude or paucity of teachings of various Sages.

The first chapter lists the Sages mentioned in the Mishnah in whose names traditions are stated. We have already mentioned at the beginning of this dissertation that the author of the Mishnah cites the names of the earliest recipients of the traditional teachings [from Sinai] beginning only with Simeon the Righteous until his generation, and the entire transmission of these teachings dates back to Simeon the Righteous. The number of these individuals in whose name all the laws and questions and decrees and edicts in the entire Mishnah were written is ninety-one, and they are the following:

1. Rabbi Eliezer ben Hyrcanus
2. Rabbi Eliezer ben Jacob
3. Rabbi Eliezer, the son of Rabbi Jose the Galilean
4. Joshua ben Perahyah
5. Rabbi Joshua ben Haninah[798]
6. Rabbi Joshua ben Karcha
7. Rabbi Joshua ben Beteyra
8. Rabbi Joshua ben Hyrcanus

9. Rabbi Elazar ben Azariah
10. Rabbi Elazar ben Judah of Bartota
11. Rabbi Elazar ben Rabbi Tzadok
12. Rabbi Elazar ben Shamua
13. Rabbi Elazar Hisma
14. Rabbi Elazar ben Parta
15. Rabbi Elazar ben Rabbi Simeon
16. Rabbi Elazar ben Piabi[799]
17. Rabbi Judah ben Rabbi Elai
18. Rabbi Judah ben Beteyra
19. Rabbi Judah ben Baba
20. Rabbi Judah ben Abba
21. Judah ben Tabbai
22. Rabbi Simeon ben Gamliel
23. Rabbi Simeon ben Yohai
24. Rabbi Simeon of Shezur
25. Rabbi Simeon ben Nanos
26. Rabbi Simeon son of the Adjutant
27. Simeon ben Shetah
28. Simeon of Timna
29. Rabbi Simeon ben Azzai
30. Rabbi Simeon ben Zoma
31. Rabbi Simeon ben Elazar
32. Rabbi Simeon ben Judah
33. Rabbi Simeon ben Beteyra
34. Simeon, brother of Azariah
35. Rabbi Hananiah, Adjutant of the Priests

36. Rabbi Hananiah ben Antigonus
37. Haninah[800] ben Hakinai
38. Rabbi Haninah[801] ben Gamliel
39. Rabbi Nehuniah ben Elnatan[802] of Kfar Bavli
40. Rabbi Ishmael
41. Rabbi Nehemiah
42. Rabbi Nehemiah of Bet Deli
43. Rabbi Yohanan ben Nuri
44. Yohanan the High Priest
45. Rabban Yohanan ben Zakkai
46. Rabbi Yohanan ben Beroka
47. Yohanan ben Gudgada
48. Rabbi Yohanan the Sandalmaker
49. Rabbi Yohanan ben Yeshua, son of the father-in-law of Rabbi Akiba
50. Rabbi Jose (ben Halafta)[803]
51. Rabbi Jose ben Meshullam
52. Rabbi Jose ben Hahotef Efrati
53. Rabbi Jose the Galilean
54. Joseph ben Joezer
55. Joseph[804] ben Yohanan
56. Rabbi Jose ben Rabbi Judah
57. Rabbi Jose the Priest
58. Jose ben Honi
59. Rabban Gamliel

60. Rabban Gamliel the Elder
61. Dosthai of Kfar Damai
62. Rabbi Dosthai ben Rabbi Yannai
63. Abba Saul
64. Rabbi Tarfon
65. Rabbi Meir
66. Rabbi Akiba
67. Rabbi Hutzpit
68. Rabbi Nathan
69. Nahum the Scribe
70. Rabbi Measha
71. Rabbi Tzadok
72. Nahum the Mede
73. Rabbi Dosa ben Horkinas
74. Rabbi Ilai
75. Ben Kuvri
76. Rabbi Papias
77. Rabbi Matiah ben Heresh
78. Nittai the Arbelite
79. Shemayah
80. Abtalion
81. Hillel
82. Shammai
83. Rabbi Zechariah ben HaKatzab
84. Admon
85. Hanan ben Avshalom

86. Rebbe[805]
87. Yadua the Babylonian
88. Akavya ben Mahallalel
89. Rabbi Yakim of Hadid
90. Menahem ben Saginai
91. Rabbi Jacob[806]

In the enumeration of these names, I have not paid attention to their chronological sequence.

The second chapter lists the Sages mentioned in the Mishnah because of an occurrence that once happened to one of them or because of an ethical teaching that he preached or because of a scriptural phrase that he expounded homiletically. There are recorded in the Mishnah names of many such Sages, not because a halakhic principle formulating prohibition or permissibility is attributed to them; rather they are mentioned because of an event that once happened to them or because he taught an ethical principle such as those Sages enumerated in tractate Avot. And thus is preserved the moral teaching or the homiletical exposition that he expounded that does not deal with the forbidden or permissible and that exposition is recorded in his name. The number of Sages whose names are mentioned because of one of the aforementioned reasons, or their like, is thirty-seven and they are as follows:

1. Rabbi Joshua ben Levi[807]
2. Rabbi Elazar HaKappar
3. Rabbi Elazar ben Arakh
4. Rabbi Elazar of Modi'im
5. Judah ben Tema
6. Rabbi Simeon ben Nathaniel
7. Rabbi Simeon ben Akashya
8. Rabbi Simeon ben Halafta
9. Haninah ben Dosa
10. Hananiah ben Hizkiah ben Goron
11. Rabbi Hananiah ben Teradion
12. Rabbi Nehunya ben HaKanah
13. Rabbi Ishmael ben Pavi
14. Yohanan ben HaHoroni
15. Rabbi Jose ben Judah of Kfar Bavli
16. Rabbi Jose ben Dormaskit
17. Rabban Gamliel, son of Rabbi Judah the Prince
18. Rabbi Simeon of HaMitzpah
19. Honi the circle drawer
20. Rabbi Hyrcanus
21. Rabbi Yannai
22. Rabbi Nehorai

23. Antigonus of Socho
24. Rabbi Halafta of Kfar Hananiah
25. Rabbi Levitas of Yavneh
26. Rabbi Jonathan
27. Samuel the Younger[808]
28. Ben Bag-Bag
29. Ben He-He
30. Elihoaynai ben Hakof
31. Hanamael the Egyptian
32. Rabbi Simeon ben Manasyah
33. Abba Saul ben Botnith
34. Zechariah ben Kabutar
35. Baba ben Buta
36. Rabbi Ishmael, the son of Rabbi Yohanan ben Beroka
37. Rabbi Ishmael, the son of Rabbi Jose

In the enumeration of these Sages as well, I have not paid attention to their chronological sequence. Therefore, the sum total of the number of Sages mentioned in the Mishnah is 128.[809]

There are two additional people mentioned in the Mishnah and they are: Elisha Aher,[810] and we do not enumerate him among these pure Sages because of the matter that is well known regarding him; and Menahem, friend of Shammai,[811] whom we have also not listed because there is absolutely nothing attributable to him in the Mishnah that adds anything to what has already been said.[812]

The third chapter deals with that which is known about the ancestry of Sages of the Mishnah. Among them are Rabban Gamliel, son of Rabbi Judah the Prince, and Rabbi Judah the Prince, son of Rabban Simeon,[813] son of Rabban Gamliel, son of Rabbi Simeon, son of Rabban Gamliel, the elder son of Rabban Simeon, son of Hillel the Prince. The latter is Hillel the Babylonian to whom a group of Sages adhered and who accepted his opinions. Therefore, it was called the school of Hillel. This Hillel is of the descendants of Shefatia, son of Avital and David.[814] It is thus clear that these seven Sages are of the seed of David.

Others in this chapter include four from among the proselytes, and these are Shemayah and Abtalion,[815] Rabbi Akiba, and Rabbi Meir. Yet others are Priests such as Simeon the Righteous, from whom originate all traditions fulfilling that which is written,[816] *They shall teach Jacob thy judgments and Israel thy law.* [Other Priests are] Rabbi Elazar ben Azariah, who is the tenth generation after Ezra and his uncle Simeon who is known as Simeon, brother of Azariah,[817] and Rabbi Elazar ben Shamua and Rabbi Haninah, Prefect of the Priests, and Rabbi Simeon, his son who is the famous Rabbi Simeon, son of the Adjutant, and Ishmael ben Pavi[818] and Yohanan the High Priest[819] and Rabban Yohanan ben Zakkai and Joseph ben Joezer and Rabbi Jose the Priest and Rabbi Tarfon Eliho'aynai ben Hakof[820] and Hanamael the Egyptian.[821] The remainder are Israelites[822] and, as far as I can remember, their ancestry is unknown.

The fourth chapter lists the Sages who lived in the same generation. Simeon the Righteous and Rabbi Dosa ben Horkinas lived in the same generation. Rabbi Dosa ben Horkinas lived to an advanced age until he reached the era of Rabbi Akiba and the people of the latter's generation and his constitutes the first generation [of talmudic Sages]. The second generation is that of Antigonus of Socho and Rabbi Elazar ben Harsom. The third generation is that of Jose ben Joezer of Tzeredah and Jose ben Yohanan of Jerusalem. The fourth generation is that of Yohanan ben Mattatias and Joshua ben Perahyah and Nittai the Arbelite. The fifth generation is that of Honi the circle drawer, and Eliho'aynai ben Hakof and Judah ben Tabbai and Simeon ben Shetah. The sixth generation is that of Akavya ben Mahallalel and Shemayah and Abtalion and Rabbi Mayashah and Hanan and Admon. The seventh generation is that of

Shammai and Hillel and Menahem and Judah ben Beteyra and Rabbi Papias and Rabbi Yohanan ben Bag-Bag and Hananiah ben Hizkiah ben Goron and Rabbi Nehuniah ben HaKanah and Baba ben Buta and Rabbi Yohanan ben HaHoroni and Rabban Gamliel the Elder and Nahum the Scribe.

These seven generations of Sages lived during the time of the Second Temple, from its beginning to its termination,[823] but they did not witness its destruction. However, the succeeding generation, which did witness the destruction of the Temple, is that of Rabbi Eliezer ben Jacob and Rabbi Tzadok and Rabbi Eliezer, his son, and Rabban Yohanan ben Zakkai and his disciples and Rabbi Ishmael ben Elisha, the High Priest, and Abba Saul and Rabbi Elazar of Modi'im and Rabbi Haninah, Adjutant of the Priests, and Rabban Gamliel and Rabbi Simeon, his son, and Rabbi Hananiah ben Antigonus and Rabbi Haninah ben Dosa and Rabbi Hananiah ben Teradion and Samuel the Younger and Rabbi Elazar ben Parta and Rabbi Elazar ben Doma and Hananiah ben Hakinai and Rabbi Judah ben Abba. The second generation after the destruction of the Temple is that of Rabbi Tarfon and Rabbi Akiba and Rabbi Elazar ben Azariah[824] and Rabbi Ishmael[825] and Rabbi Joshua ben Karcha and Hananiah of Onno and

Simeon ben Nanos and Yohanan ben Beroka and his son Rabbi Ishmael and Rabbi Yohanan ben Gudgada and Rabbi Elazar Hisma and Rabbi Judah ben Tema. The third generation is that of Rabbi Meir and Rabbi Judah and Rabbi Jose and Rabbi Nathan and Rabbi Yohanan the Sandalmaker and Rabbi Jose the Galilean and his son, Rabbi Elazar, and Rabbi Elazar ben Shamua and Simeon ben Azzai and Simeon ben Zoma and Rabbi Hutzpit, the translator. The fourth generation [of Sages after the destruction of the Temple] is that of Rabbi Judah the Prince and his sons, Rabban Gamliel and Rabbi Simeon, and Rabbi Simeon ben Yohai and his son Rabbi Elazar and Rabbi Simeon ben Elazar and Rabbi Ishmael, son of Rabbi Jose, and Rabbi Jonathan. This generation is the last of the Sages of the Mishnah.

The fifth chapter elucidates, as far as is known, who is the disciple and who is the teacher. We have already mentioned at the beginning of our remarks[826] that Rebbe, redactor of the Mishnah, was a disciple of his father. Similarly, each of his predecessors was a student of his respective father, going all the way back to Hillel and to Simeon the Righteous, as we have mentioned. So, too, Rabban Yohanan ben Zakkai was a pupil of Hillel and the pupils of Rabban Yohanan ben Zakkai were five:

Rabbi Eliezer ben Hyrcanus, whose story is known,[827] and Rabbi Joshua ben Haninah and Rabbi Jose the Priest and Rabbi Simeon ben Nathaniel and Rabbi Elazer ben Arakh. This is the group that received the good tidings [from God] that they would partake of the life of the world to come, as is expounded in the Talmud,[828] they and their disciples and their disciples' disciples. And Rabbi Akiba was the pupil of Rabbi Eliezer ben Hyrcanus, and the latter was his distinguished teacher. Rabbi Akiba also learned a little from Rabbi Tarfon, but the latter was not considered his teacher but his colleague. And Rabbi Akiba honored Rabbi Tarfon by calling him "Rebbe"[829] and Rabbi Tarfon called Rabbi Akiba "Akiba."[830] And we find that Rabbi Akiba said to him, "Give me permission to state before you something that you have taught me," as it explained in *Sifra*.[831] And Rabbi Meir and Rabbi Simeon ben Yohai were disciples of Rabbi Akiba and he was their distinguished teacher. And Rabbi Meir also studied under Rabbi Ishmael and others.[832] And Rabbi Judah studied under Rabbi Elazar ben Azariah, who was his distinguished teacher. Wherever one finds in the Mishnah "Rabbi so and so, in the name of Rabbi so and so" – know that the former is the latter's disciple and, therefore, accepted his viewpoint. And Rabbi Judah the Prince also studied under Rabbi Elazar ben Shamua.[833] Sumchus was a disciple of Rabbi Meir and wished to study under Rabbi Judah after Rabbi Meir's death, but it was not so.[834]

The sixth chapter seeks to disclose hidden names[835] and to aid in their identification. Rabbi Eliezer, when mentioned anonymously in the Mishnah, refers to Rabbi Eliezer ben Hyrcanus, disciple of Rabban Yohanan ben Zakkai. Rabbi Joshua, when mentioned anonymously, refers to Rabbi Joshua ben Haninah, disciple of Rabban Yohanan ben Zakkai. And Rabbi Judah, when mentioned anonymously, refers to Rabbi Judah ben Ilai of whom it is stated in the Talmud, "It once happened with a certain pious man,"[836] and this is the name by which he is known to them. Rabbi Elazar, when stated anonymously, refers to Rabbi Elazar ben Shamua the Priest who lived in the generation of Rabban Gamliel. It was from him that Rebbe wished to learn but his[837] disciples did not allow him[838] to learn from him save a little.[839] And Rabbi Simeon, when mentioned anonymously, refers to Rabbi Simeon ben Yohai disciple of Rabbi Akiba; the story involving him and the Emperor is well known.[840] And Rabbi Elazar ben Rabbi Simeon is his son. Ben Azai and

Ben Zoma and Ben Nannas refer to Simeon ben Azzai and Simeon ben Zoma and Simeon ben Nannas. Ben Beteyra is Rabbi Joshua ben Beteyra and Ben Bag-Bag refers to Rabbi Yohanan ben Bag-Bag. And Yohanan the High Priest refers to the famous Yohanan ben Mattathias, who is mentioned in the prayers dealing with our victory over the Greek kings.[841]

Once Rabbi Meir and Rabbi Nathan wished to embarrass Rabban Simeon, the father of Rebbe, concerning a matter that is described in great detail[842] and Rabban Simeon expelled them from his rabbinical college. And if a legal decision is enunciated in one of their names, if in the name of Rabbi Meir, it is reported as "others state," and if in the name of Rabbi Nathan, it is reported as "some say."[843] However, when it says in the Mishnah, "A disciple in the name of Rabbi Ishmael stated in the presence of Rabbi Akiba,"[844] it refers to Rabbi Meir. Also, that which the Sages stated, "It was discussed before the Sages,"[845] refers to five people: Rabbi Simeon ben Azzai, Rabbi Simeon ben Zoma, Rabbi Simeon ben Nannas,[846] Hanan [the Egyptian], and Hananiah of Onno.[847] And Rabbi Meir is also called Rabbi Nehorai, and both are one and the same,[848] but his original name was Rabbi Nehemiah.[849]

That which is mentioned in the Mishnah "Sages" [has various connotations]. Sometimes the term *Sages* refers to one of the Sages whose name was mentioned earlier; sometimes it refers to the entire multitude of Sages; many times the Talmud itself explains by asking, to whom does "Sages" refer? and answers "Rabbi so and so." And this[850] is done when there are many Sages who agree with the viewpoint of that Sage. And because those who accept that viewpoint are many, they are called "Sages" even though the teaching itself stems from a single Sage. However, when it says "School[851] of Shammai" and "School[852] of Hillel," it refers to the group of Sages who accept the opinion of Shammai and the group of Sages who accept the opinion of Hillel, for the disciples of a person are like members of his household. "Rebbe" refers to our Holy Rabbi who is Rabbi Judah the Prince–the sixth generation from Hillel the Elder–and he is the compiler of the Mishnah.

Wherever it states in the Mishnah, "They said in truth," this refers to a legal principle given to Moses at Sinai.[853] An anonymous mishnah is one in which the majority viewpoint is accepted, where deliberations reached a common viewpoint, and where there is no difference of opinion; or it refers to a tradition transmitted from group to group going back until Moses, as we have described at the beginning of this dissertation. The last to receive that teaching and to whom it is, therefore, attributed is Rabbi Meir and this is what is meant by the statement, "An anonymous mishnah represents the view of Rabbi Meir."[854] Aside from some of the anonymous ones that may be Rabbi Meir's own opinions, against which others offer differing viewpoints, some may represent views of a Sage other than Rabbi Meir, but then the Talmud identifies him.[855] When I pronounce a final legal decision according to whomever it may be in any legal matter of all those in the Mishnah, you will find your answer in that matter.[856]

The seventh chapter mentions the seniority of the Sages according to the ranking of the author [of the Mishnah, Rebbe]. He subdivided into three levels the standings of the 128 Sages cited in the Mishnah as we mentioned earlier. Those who he considered extremely distinguished and on the highest level he called by their names [only][857] such as Hillel and Shammai and Shemaya and Abtalion because of the greatness of their status since it is impossible to find a title appropriate to exalt their name, just as there are no titles for the prophets.[858] Those Sages whom he considered to be below this level he designated with the term

Rabban such as Rabban Gamliel and Rabban Yohanan ben Zakkai.[859] Those whom he considered to be below this level, he called "Rabbi" such as Rabbi Meir and Rabbi Judah.[860] He also gave people on this level the appellation "Abba," as for example Abba Saul.[861] Sometimes he omitted the title – and one should not be concerned [that this may detract from their honor] – as when he stated Simeon brother of Azariah[862] and Elazar of Bartota. Among those whom he called by name only as a sign of honor are the following: Simeon the Righteous, Antigonus of Socho, Jose ben Joezer, Jose ben Yohanan, Yohanan the High Priest, Joshua ben Perahyah, Nittai the Arbelite, Honi the circle drawer, Elyeho'aynai ben Hakof, Hanamael the Egyptian, Judah ben Tabbai, Simeon ben Shetah, Akavya ben Mahallalel, Shemaya and Abtalion, Hanan and Admon, Hillel and Shammai, Nahum the Scribe, Hananiah ben Hizkiah ben Goron, and Baba ben Buta. Anyone mentioned by name only, other than the above, had his title omitted [by Rebbe] but it is of no consequence.[863]

The eighth chapter associates [various Sages with] certain places, professions, persons, and families. To all these recipients of the tradition, the author of the Mishnah often adds an explanatory term. Some he associates with their profession so that it be known such as "Nahum the Scribe" or "Rabbi Simeon the weaver." Others he associates with their native land as when he says "man from Hadid" or "man from Ono" or "man from Bartota." When he declares "from Tzereda" and "from Jerusalem"[864] and other names of places, he means to say that that Sage is the wise man of that town and the most distinguished as if to say that that man who is an inhabitant of that town is truly worthy to be called "man from." Other Sages are described by using their father's or brother's name such as "Rabbi so and so, son of so and so" or "Rabbi so and so, brother of so and so," and there are many examples of this type. Others he makes known through their families such as when he states "so and so the Priest."

The ninth chapter lists those Sages among whom differences of opinion occur in most of their discussions. The people in the Mishnah among whom argumentation occurs in most instances are the following: Rabbi Meir and Rabbi Judah and Rabbi Simeon and Rabbi Jose. Among these four, there are frequently disputes between any pair of them and also among all four. One also finds Rabbi Elazer arguing with each of the above four but less frequently than the argumentation that occurs among the four. Similarly, in regard to

Rabbi Akiba and Rabbi Eliezer and Rabbi Joshua,one finds disputes among each of them and among all three but their differences of opinion are less frequent than those of the aforementioned four Sages. And one also finds disputes between Rabbi Akiba and Rabbi Ishmael and Rabbi Tarfon and Rabbi Elazar ben Azariah, but less frequently than among the aforementioned group. After them in decreasing frequency of disputes are the School of Shammai and the School of Hillel. The least amount of controversy is found between Rabban Gamliel or Rabban Simeon ben Gamliel or Rebbe with any one of the aforementioned Sages. Most of the differences of opinion in the Mishnah occur among these Sages, with few exceptions.[865]

The tenth chapter deals with the multitude or paucity of teachings of various Sages. Among the Sages who received [and transmitted] the Mishnah, as we have described, are some in whose names many legal decisions are stated, such as Rabbi Meir and Rabbi Judah. There are others in whose names very few legal decisions are written, such as Rabbi Eliezer ben Jacob, as it is stated, "The teaching of Rabbi Eliezer ben Jacob is little, but pure,"[866] that is to say his teachings are few but the final ruling is in accordance with his viewpoint in all cases. In keeping with what we have mentioned in the previous chapter, the multitude or paucity of teachings of the various Sages is directly related to the multitude or paucity of argumentations of these Sages.[867] There are some Sages in whose name only a single legal ruling is written in the Mishnah and whose name is not repeated again in relation to any legal matter in the Torah.[868] There are thirty-eight such individuals:

(1) Nahum the Scribe and (2) Rabbi Measha, only in Tractate Pe'ah,[869] and there is not a second statement by them at all in any other place.

(3) Hananiah ben Hahinai and (4) Rabbi Joseph ben HaHotef Efrati only in tractate Kilayim.[870]

(5) Rabbi Elazar Hisma and (6) Rabbi Jose ben Meshulam only in tractate Terumot.[871]

(7) Rabbi Hutzpit only in tractate Shevi'it.[872]

(8) Rabbi Elazar ben Judah of Bartota and (9) Dosthai of Kfar Damai only in tractate Orlah.[873]

(10) Nahum the Mede only in tractate Shabbat.[874]

(11) Rabbi Ilai and (12) Rabbi Dosthai son of Rabbi Yannai only in tractate Eruvin.[875]

(13) Rabbi Simeon son of the Adjutant to the

priests and (14) Ben Bukri only in tractate Shekalim.[876]

(15) Judah ben Tabbai and (16) Simeon ben Shetah and

(17) Jose ben Joezer and (18) Jose ben Yohanan and (19) Nittai the Arbelite and (20) Joshua ben Perahyah only in tractate Hagigah.[877]

(21) Simeon of Timna and (22) Nehemiah of Bet Deli only in tractate Yevamot.[878]

(23) Rabbi Eliezer son of Rabbi Jose the Galilean and

(24) Rabbi Joshua ben Hyrcanus only in tractate Sotah.[879]

(25) Yadua the Babylonian only in tractate Bava Metzia.[880]

(26) Rabbi Simeon ben Judah only in tractate Shevu'ot.[881]

(27) Rabbi Simeon ben Beteyra and (28) Rabbi Nehuniah ben Elnatan of Kfar Bavli and (29) Rabbi Jose the Priest and (30) Rabbi Yakim of Hadid and (31) Menahem ben Saginai only in tractate Eduyot.[882]

(32) Simeon brother of Azariah[883] and (33) Jose ben Honi only in tractate Zevahim.[884]

(34) Rabbi Elazar son of Rabbi Simeon only in tractate Temurah.[885]

(35) Rabbi Jacob only in tractate Nega'im.[886]

(36) Abba Elazar ben Delayi only in tractate Mikva'ot.[887]

(37) Rabbi Elazar ben Piabi only in tractate Tohorot.[888]

(38) Rabbi Yohanan ben Joshua, son of Rabbi Akiba's father-in-law, only in tractate Yadayim.[889]

None of these people that we have enumerated is cited more than once in all the laws of the Mishnah in the tractates we have listed.[890]

And I have thus completed my introductory remarks, and I will now commence with the commentary as I promised.

Notes

1. The introduction to Seder Zera'im is preceded by an introductory poem. The idea of a prefatory poem to a religious work or text was a very common medieval device. It was used by such famous writers as Ibn Ezra and Yehuda Halevy. The nature of Maimonides' introductory poem to Seder Zera'im is that it is replete with biblical paraphrases, and does not try to create its own free image of expression. The poem molds established biblical texts into itself. It is impossible to translate this Hebrew poem without injustice, among other things, to all the allusions. To the person reading the poem in the Hebrew, these allusions are clear from the original biblical texts. The English reader may not recognize the allusions, although the footnotes point them out.

One of the medieval literary ornaments to religious writings is the use of metrical patterns in these introductory poems. Many of these patterns were borrowed from the Arabic. A specific metrical pattern does not seem to have been employed in Maimonides' introductory poem; rather it is written in free verse rhythm. No attempt was made in the English translation to maintain the rhyme present in the Hebrew version.

2. Probably derived from Daniel 10:11.

3. Psalms 34:12.

4. Isaiah 55:2.

5. Psalms 34:13.

6. Derived from Ecclesiastes 9:14, where the "great king" refers to the evil inclination of man.

7. Derived from Daniel 1:8.

8. Derived from Proverbs 9:5.

9. Derived from Song of Songs 7:14.

10. Ibid., 8:2.

11. Ibid., 7:10.

12. Or corn. Derived from Deuteronomy 18:4.

13. Derived from Isaiah 21:10. Maimonides is poetically describing his Mishnah Commentary as his "first fruits," etc.

14. Isaiah 5:1. Lit.: "a horn the son of fatness," an allusion to the fertility of the land of Israel.

15. Psalms 78:25.

16. Numbers 11:8.

17. Nehemiah 8:10.

18. Song of Songs 5:1.

19. Ezekiel 41:22.

20. Legislative prohibitions decreed by Rabbis in certain times to "protect" various rules of the Torah.

21. Isaiah 40:11.

22. The Commentary.

23. Sages.

24. Numbers 15:23.

25. Song of Songs 4:4.

26. Derived from Jeremiah 41:16.

27. Song of Songs 4:4.

28. I.e., composed the Commentary.

29. Sages of the post-Talmud era.

30. Derived from Isaiah 23:18.

31. This introduction to tractate Berakhot serves as the general introduction to the entire *Commentary on the Mishnah*. It is sometimes spoken of as the introduction to Seder Zera'im since Maimonides wrote separate introductions for the other sections or orders of the Mishnah.

32. Lit.: peace be upon him.

33. Eruvin 54b.

34. This oral transmittal of precepts and their explanation comprise the "Oral Law": (*Torah She-B'al Peh*) and is extant today as the Talmud (Mishnah and Gemara). This is in contradistinction to the "written Law" (*Torah She-Bikhetav*), which is the Pentateuch.

35. *Torat Kohanim*, a halakhic commentary on Leviticus 26:54.

36. Leviticus 25:1.

37. Lit.: said.

38. Resting of the soil and cancellation of debts in the Sabbatical year.

39. Leviticus 23:42.

40. Booth or hut or tabernacle.

41. Deuteronomy 1:3.

42. Deuteronomy 1:5.

43. Maimonides explains *Beraita, Sifra* and *Sifre* later in his Introduction to the Commentary.

44. *Sifre*, Deuteronomy 1:5.

NOTES

45. One month and seven days.

46. Lit.: books.

47. The first word in the Torah.

48. The last three words in the Torah; they begin and end with the letter *lamed*. See Bava Batra 15a.

49. Deuteronomy 31:26.

50. Lit.: half.

51. *Sifre* Deuteronomy 32:47.

52. Megillah 13b and Kiddushin 38a.

53. *Sifre* Deuteronomy 32:48.

54. Sotah 13b and *Sifre* Deuteronomy 34:34.

55. Questions whose answers can be derived from the explicit law.

56. *Sifra* 1, also known as the *Beraita* of Rabbi Ishmael, which enunciates the thirteen principles of rabbinic exegesis. See Hertz, *Authorized Daily Prayer Book* (New York: Bloch Publishers, 1959), p. 43.

57. Between two biblical laws.

58. Exodus 23:2.

59. Compilers of the Gemara of the Babylonian Talmud.

60. Lit.: let my soul live; an expression of oath common among the prophets.

61. Lit.: imagining in their souls.

62. Lit.: until.

63. Lit.: sign.

64. 1 Kings 17:21.

65. Disciple of Elijah the prophet. See 2 Kings 4:1–37.

66. Job 22:28.

67. 1 Kings 18:28.

68. See Deuteronomy 13:3.
69. I.e., if they forewarned him.
70. Deuteronomy 13:6.
71. *Sifre* Deuteronomy 13:6.
72. Deuteronomy 13:4.
73. Alternate translation: all that is found.
74. The false prophet.
75. Lit.: uncircumcised. The fruit of newly planted trees is to be rejected for the first three years.
76. Ibid.
77. Leviticus 19:23.
78. Deuteronomy 23:12 and *Sifre* there.
79. Exodus 19:9.
80. Deuteronomy 30:12.
81. Deuteronomy 30:14.
82. The precepts of the Torah.
83. Deuteronomy 13:1.
84. Megillah 2b.
85. Deuteronomy 18:20.
86. Malachi 3:22.
87. 1 Samuel 15:3.
88. The King of Israel.
89. 2 Kings 6:22.
90. Isaiah 22:9–10.
91. Jeremiah 42:15 or ibid., 29:4–9.
92. Lit.: testimony.
93. The true prophet.
94. As distinguished from a death meted out by a human court.
95. Deuteronomy 18:19.

96. Alternate translation: faith.

97. Shabbat 92a. Strong in character and rich in being contented with his lot.

98. If he fulfills the above criteria.

99. Deuteronomy 18:21.

100. 1 Samuel 3:20.

101. Ibid., 3:9.

102. Lit.: stargazers.

103. Deuteronomy 18:14–15.

104. 1 Samuel 9:9. See also Maimonides' *Guide for the Perplexed* 2:38.

105. Lit.: possessors of spiritual powers.

106. Lit.: may God live; an expression of oath.

107. Derived from Job 21:29.

108. Isaiah 47:13.

109. Genesis Rabbah 85:3. The Sages deduced that the phrase *from the* meant to exclude the possibility of *all the*. This is a typical hermeneutic deduction.

110. A prophet's.

111. Lit.: fall.

112. 2 Kings 10:10

113. Jeremiah 23:28.

114. Berakhot 55a.

115. The people for whom ill was predicted.

116. Lit.: a different time.

117. 1 Kings 21:29.

118. See note 115.

119. Deuteronomy 18:22.

120. Ibid.

121. Lit.: his spirit filled him.

122. Lit.: definitely.

123. Berakhot 7a. The meaning of this phrase is that if God promises something conditionally, if the condition is obeyed, He will not change it, although the original condition may have weakened His commitment.
124. Genesis 28:15.
125. Ibid., 32:7.
126. Berakhot 4a.
127. Deuteronomy 18:22.
128. Jeremiah, Chapter 28.
129. Ibid.
130. Hananiah.
131. The Jewish people.
132. Jeremiah.
133. Jeremiah 28:7–9.
134. "Thou shalt . . ." or "thou shalt not . . . ."
135. Shortening of one's natural life span.
136. Sanhedrin 90a.
137. Hebrew: *Bet Din*. Lit.: house of judgment or law.
138. 1 Kings 18:31–40.
139. Divine punishment by either sudden or premature death, or by inability to procreate.
140. Deuteronomy 12:13.
141. *Karet*. See note 139, above.
142. Leviticus 17:4 or ibid. 17:9.
143. Lit.: to nullify their claims.
144. 2 Kings 3:19.
145. Deuteronomy 20:19.
146. Lit.: commanded.
147. The prophet.
148. Deuteronomy 18:15.
149. Sanhedrin 90a.

150. Lit.: make incense.

151. Lit.: to fulfill this command.

152. As opposed to a human court.

153. The prophet.

154. Deuteronomy 18:19.

155. A prohibited principal labor on the Sabbath. See Shabbat 111b.

156. Hebrew: *Tehum Shabbat,* the area around a town or place within which it is permitted to walk on the Sabbath two thousand cubits in each direction. Based on Exodus 16:29.

157. Exodus 23:2.

158. Hullin 124a.

159. The ceremony of taking off the shoe of the brother of a husband who died childless and who does not want to or cannot fulfill the Levirate marriage. Based on Deuteronomy 23:5–9.

160. Made of soft leather and covering the upper part of the foot.

161. According to Rashi and other commentators this text should read: "were he to declare that *Halitzah* may not be performed with a sandal, he would not be obeyed."

162. Yevamot 102a.

163. Moses.

164. Deuteronomy 30:12.

165. Ibid., 17:9.

166. Bava Metzia 59b.

167. Lit.: taught.

168. Joshua 24:31.

169. Lit.: there was not time.

170. Lit.: words.

171. Lit.: accepted or transmitted.

172. Approximately the fifth century B.C.E. The last Head of this Assembly was Simeon the righteous.

173. 2 Kings 24:16 and Gittin 88a.

174. Lit.: pure.

175. The Sages of the Mishnah, also called *Tanna'im*.

176. Rabbi Judah the Patriarch, Our Holy Rabbi.

177. He was supreme in both Torah and secular matters. Gittin 59a.

178. Sotah 49a. Although this statement is in the Mishnah, it must have been added later since Rebbe himself compiled the Mishnah.

179. Holy tongue.

180. Lit.: letters.

181. Lit.: about which they were doubtful.

182. Rosh Hashanah 26b.

183. Some texts add: "and great capabilities."

184. Bava Metzia 85a. King Shapur the First reigned over Persia in the third century.

185. In his introduction to the *Mishneh Torah* (Code of Maimonides), he continues the lineage as follows: "Jeremiah from Zephaniah, Zephaniah from Habbakuk, Habbakuk from Nahum, Nahum from Joel, Joel from Mikah, Mikah from Isaiah, Isaiah from Amos, Amos from Hosea, Hosea from Zechariah, Zechariah from Jehojadah, Jehojadah from Elisha, Elisha from Elijah, Elijah from Ahiyah, Ahiyah from David, David from Samuel, Samuel from Eli, Eli from Pinhas, Pinhas from Joshua, Joshua from Moses our teacher, Moses our teacher, the teacher of all prophets,

from the Eternal, God of Israel." Thus from Rav Ashi, compiler of the Gemara, through Rebbe, redactor of the Mishnah, until Moses, there were forty generations.

186. Rebbe, compiler of the Mishnah.

187. Chapter 1:6.

188. Lit.: *Halakhah* of Moses from Sinai.

189. Lit.: you should know it.

190. Lit.: takes out.

191. Exodus 21:24, Leviticus 24:20, and Deuteronomy 19:21.

192. Leviticus 23:40.

193. A type of citrus fruit used together with the festive wreath on the Festival of Sukkot (Booths).

194. Leviticus 23:40.

195. Hebrew: *Hadas.*

196. Deuteronomy 25:12.

197. Leviticus 21:9.

198. The Gemara in Sanhedrin 50a–51b has a lengthy discussion as to whether this edict refers to an engaged or married woman, but all agree that the scriptural verse refers to infidelity on the part of a priest's daughter who has marital ties.

199. Deuteronomy 22:20–21.

200. *Beraita* in *Torat Kohanim.*

201. Hebrew: *Asmachta*, scriptural text used as a support for a rabbinical enactment; intimation.

202. Leviticus 23:40.

203. Sukkah 35a.

204. The Hebrew word *Eitz* means both "wood" and "tree."

205. See note 204.

206. Hebrew: *Hadar*, meaning "good."

207. Hebrew: *Hadar*, meaning "lives or dwells," deduced from the infinitive *Ladur*, which means to live.

208. Greek: *Hydros*, meaning "water."

209. See note 193.

210. Date palm, one of the components of the festive wreath.

211. Sukkah 32a.

212. Bava Kamma 83b.

213. Sanhedrin 52a.

214. The thirteen principles of rabbinic exegesis. See Hertz, *Authorized Daily Prayer Book* (New York: Bloch, 1959), p. 43.

215. Lit.: *Halakhah* to Moses from Sinai, i.e., traditional interpretation of a written law.

216. Lit.: through one of the (thirteen) principles.

217. Berakhot 41a, Eruvin 4a, and Sukkah 5b.

218. Deuteronomy 8:8.

219. I.e., this biblical phrase only enumerates types of fruit, but does not mean to give measurements.

220. E.g., Sukkah 6a.

221. Verbal Mosaic Traditions.

222. A liquid measure equal to the contents or space occupied by six eggs.

223. Leviticus 7:12.

224. Numbers 6:15.

225. Menahot 89a.

226. Hebrew: *Gud*. A wall that does not reach the floor or ceiling is considered "extended" as if touching the floor or ceiling.

227. Hebrew: *Levud*. A wall with holes or gaps less than

three handbreadths is considered "solidified" or "filled in" by disregarding the holes or gaps.

228. Hebrew: *Akuma*. If part of the roof near one of the walls of a *Sukkah* is made of prohibited materials, then the wall is considered "curved" or "bent" toward the permitted roof materials, and the *Sukkah* is proper for use.

229. Sukkah 6b.

230. Such as eating food equivalent to the size of an olive regarding the requirement of reciting Grace after Meals.

231. Things that intervene between the body and the ritual immersion water that invalidate the ritual bath.

232. A height of at least ten handbreadths is required.

233. Eruvin 4a and Sukkah 3b.

234. Sukkah 34a and 48a; Taanit 3a; Mo'ed Katan 3b; and Zevahim 110b. This sentence is lacking in some texts.

235. Hebrew: *K'laf*.

236. The inscription on the door post containing Deuteronomy 6:4–9, 11:13–21.

237. Hebrew: *Duksustos*, or inner portion of the parchment.

238. Hebrew: *Gevil*, or outer layer of hide when it is split, or vellum.

239. Shabbat 79b.

240. Twenty-first letter of the Hebrew alphabet.

241. Written on the exterior of the box.

242. They must form a cube; they may not be round or rectangular.

243. Through which the straps are passed.

244. Shabbat 28b and Menahot 35a.

245. Both hair and tendons must come from a ritually clean animal.

246. See note 245.
247. Shabbat 28 and 108a.
248. Shabbat 103b and Megillah 16b.
249. I.e., she is still permitted to marry into the priesthood.
250. Niddah 45a.
251. Lit.: makes.
252. Corner of the field to be left for the poor and stranger. Leviticus 19:9. and 23:22.
253. Pe'ah 2:5.
254. Such as turnip seed or parsley seed. These seeds are extremely small and thin, and therefore unfit to eat.
255. Forbidden admixtures of seeds. Leviticus 19:19.
256. A *Se'ah* is a standard measure of area comprising 2,500 square cubits. Six *Kabbim* make up one *Se'ah*. Thus, here, garden seeds that are very thin and small require more room to grow than wheat, and only one and a half *Kabbim* can be sown in one *Se'ah*'s space. One twenty-fourth of this, or one-sixteenth of a Kab of garden seeds, if mixed into a *Se'ah* of wheat, will render it *Kilayim*.
257. Kilayim 2:2.
258. To prevent the saplings from withering.
259. Shevi'it 1:6.
260. Although one cannot usually take Heave Offering from clean for unclean, here there is no liquid such as dew, water, wine, oil, blood, milk, or bee's honey, which would predispose edibles to defilement.
261. Terumot 2:1.
262. See note 75 above. Orlah 3:9 and Kiddushin 38b. Omitted in some texts.
263. Synagogue beadle or schoolmaster or supervisor.

Today the word *Hazzan* denotes synagogue reader or cantor.

264. On Friday night, lest he forget what day it is and tilt a lamp for brighter light, thereby transgressing the Sabbath.

265. Shabbat 11a.

266. Because it is quite common for it to become reversed, and she knew of this beforehand.

267. Shabbat 92b.

268. Because it improves the wine but not vice versa, since diluting wine after having agreed to supply concentrated wine constitutes fraud.

269. Bava Metzia 60a.

270. I.e., Sabbatical.

271. Amon and Moab, countries conquered by Moses, were initially sanctified together with Israel itself. After the second Temple, however, these were excluded, and laws of the Sabbatical year, applicable to Israel, no longer applied for Amon and Moab. Jews in these countries were permitted to cultivate their fields during this year, but were required to give the poor tithe in addition to the yearly first tithe. See Yevamot 16a.

272. Hagigah 3b and Yadayim 4:3.

273. There are additional Verbal Mosaic Traditions in the Talmud that Maimonides does not enumerate here. One example is in Nedarim 37b where R. Isaac states: "Textual reading [of the Torah] and stylistic improvements as transmitted through the *Sofrim*; words read but not written and words written but not read are all Verbal Mosaic Traditions." There are also some additional ones that Maimonides describes in his *Mishneh Torah* (Code of Maimonides) but which he does not enumerate here. One

example is found in the laws of the Sanctification of the New Moon, Chapter 5, Law 2, where Maimonides states: "The following is a Verbal Mosaic Tradition: At times when there is a Sanhedrin, declaration of the New Moon is based on visual observation whereas at times that no Sanhedrin exists, it is based on calculation . . ."

274. Lit.: from the mouth of Moses.

275. Through one of the thirteen principles of rabbinic exegesis.

276. Lit.: speak of it.

277. See note 275.

278. I.e., received by tradition.

279. Yevamot 76b. In other words, if this law is one of those received from Moses that is alluded to in Scripture, or a Verbal Mosaic Tradition, we will accept it. However, if it is a law derived only through logical reasoning, we can argue thereon.

280. See note 278.

281. Lit.: the second.

282. The aforementioned thinkers.

283. I.e., insufficiently studied the Torah.

284. I.e., many conflicting rulings arose. Sanhedrin 88b and Sotah 47b.

285. I.e., faulty or damaging.

286. Berakhot 51b.

287. Lit.: the house.

288. Referring to the latter water before Grace.

289. Bet Shammai hold the former, Bet Hillel the latter.

290. Berakhot 52b.

291. Hebrew: *Am HaAretz* or ignoramus.

292. See note 283.

293. Lit.: falls between them.

294. I.e., controversy and dispute between two such people.

295. Each can only discuss at a level of intelligence with which God endowed him.

296. The disciples of Hillel and Shammai.

297. Such as Joshua and Pinchas.

298. I.e., to think derogatorily of Sages because their predecessors were more learned than they.

299. Deuteronomy 17:9.

300. See note 276.

301. A rabbinic prohibition to protect a person from transgressing a biblical injunction.

302. Leviticus 18:30.

303. Yevamot 21a; i.e., add restrictions to safeguard the original precepts. There is a play on words here. The Hebrew word *Shomor* means to observe but also means to protect.

304. Hebrew: *Gezerot*.

305. Such as cows.

306. Such as a deer. Many manuscripts and some texts substitute flesh of clean animals for cattle and beasts.

307. I.e., one should not erroneously eat cattle flesh with milk by comparing it with flesh of fowl, which is permitted in the Torah.

308. Shabbat 130a.

309. Avodah Zarah 36a.

310. Lit.: given.

311. Both are prohibited in Deuteronomy 4:2.

312. Lit.: for the fixing of the world.

313. Lit.: words.

314. Hebrew: *Takanot.*

315. I.e., social reforms.

316. Ecclesiastes 10:8.

317. Lit.: money matters.

318. Lit.: ask and seek.

319. Megillah 4a.

320. The first benediction of the Grace after Meals. Hertz *Prayer Book* (see footnote 56) p. 967.

321. Berakhot 48b.

322. Such as Bava Kamma 80b.

323. Such as Bava Kamma 82a.

324. Sheviit 10:3. *Pruzbul* is a device that prevents remission of debts in the Sabbatical year by entrusting the court with the collection of the debt. A complete discussion of *Pruzbul* can be found in Gittin 36a–37b.

325. Gittin 34b. A man should write his true name on a divorce document and not an adopted name.

326. (a) Betzah 5a. Testimony concerning the appearance of the New Moon is admitted the whole day, even in the evening. (b) Rosh Hashanah 30b. During the whole day of the waving of the *Omer* (the sheaf of barley offered on the 16th of *Nisan* prior to which new cereals of that year were forbidden. Leviticus 23:10), the new corn is forbidden.

327. As opposed to an individual Sage.

328. Ketubot 49b. A man must sustain his sons and daughters while they are young.

329. Using the thirteen principles of rabbinic exegesis.

330. Hebrew: *Gezerot.*

331. Hebrew: *Takanot.*

332. Hebrew: *Shemu'ot.*

333. As in the Code of Jewish Law, the *Shulhan Arukh.*

334. Lit.: received, by oral tradition.

335. Lit.: known to us.

336. Eduyot 1:6.

337. Rebbe, compiler of the Mishnah.

338. See note 337.

339. I.e., logical and understandable.

340. Lit.: listened to.

341. Eduyot 1:5.

342. Ibid., Mishnah 4 and Mishnah 12.

343. Such as Bet Shammai and Bet Hillel.

344. The dissenter.

345. Lit.: hard-necked.

346. Deuteronomy 16:20.

347. Avot 5:7.

348. Lit.: save your soul.

349. I.e., admit defeat with dignity.

350. As described above.

351. Hebrew: *Kilayim*. Prohibitions of mixtures in plants, animals, and garments.

352. Lit.: Uncircumcised. Prohibition of the use of trees during the first three years after planting.

353. To the Priest, Levite, poor, stranger, etc.

354. Different for each holiday.

355. The ceremony of taking off the shoe of the brother of a husband who died childless who does not want or cannot fulfill the Levirate marriage. Deuteronomy 25: 5-9.

356. Hebrew: *Ketubah*.

357. Lit.: involvements in business.

358. I.e., defilements.

359. Hebrew word meaning order.

360. Order of Seeds.

361. Order of Festivals.

362. Order of Women.

363. Order of Damages.

364. Order of Holy Things.

365. Order of Purifications.

366. The first letters of the six Orders of the Mishnah (Z–Zera'im; M–Mo'ed; N–Nashim; N–Nezikin; K–Kodashim; T–Tohorot) form the two Hebrew words "Zeman-Nakat" meaning "kept time." The names for the Orders of the Mishnah are also alluded to in Isaiah 33:6. See also Shabbat 31a.

367. Rebbe, compiler of the Mishnah.

368. I.e., produce.

369. See note 367.

370. Exodus 23:10–11.

371. Ibid., 23:12.

372. Ibid., 23:14.

373. Ibid., 21:7.

374. Ibid., 21:22.

375. Ibid., 21:28.

376. See note 367.

377. Leviticus 9:1ff., whereas sacrifices are described in the first eight chapters of Leviticus.

378. I.e., each Order or Seder.

379. Hebrew: *Masekhet*, possibly meaning either "take heed" (Deuteronomy 27:9) or "web" (Judges 16:13).

380. Hebrew: *Perek*, meaning "limb," a section or part of the whole tractate.

381. Legal decision or final ruling.

382. Order of Seeds.

383. Lit.: benedictions. Deals with prayers, worship, and benedictions.

384. Rebbe, compiler of the Mishnah.

385. Berakhot 35a.

386. First Mishnah in Berakhot.

387. Lit.: corners. Deals with corners of fields to be left to the poor.

388. Lit.: gifts.

389. I.e., harvest.

390. Hebrew: doubtful. Produce over which a doubt exists as to whether it was tithed or not. He who buys such produce must remove tithe therefrom, except the poor who are exempt.

391. The Sages.

392. Demai 3:1.

393. Hebrew: mixtures. Deals with prohibitions of mixtures of plants, animals, and garments.

394. Lit.: Order.

395. Leviticus 19:2.

396. Leviticus 19:9.

397. Leviticus 19:19.

398. Hebrew: Sabbatical or seventh. Deals with laws of the Sabbatical year.

399. Hebrew: Uncircumcised or foreskin. Deals with the prohibition of the use of the fruit of trees for the first three years after planting.

400. Leviticus 19:23.

401. Leviticus 23:1ff.

402. Hebrew: Heave offering. Deals with laws of the Heave offering.

403. This is then given to the Priest.
404. Hebrew: First Tithe given to the Levite. Numbers 18:21–32.
405. Hebrew: Second Tithe brought to Jerusalem and eaten by the owner. Deuteronomy 14:22.
406. Either their sequence in the Torah or their importance. *Maaser Sheni* is brought two of three years, whereas *Maaser Rishon* is brought three of five years; more frequent and more important.
407. Deals with laws pertaining to the portions of dough to be given to the Priest. The word *hallah* is untranslatable. The Hebrew word for dough is *Issah*.
408. Hebrew: First Fruits.
409. Leviticus 19:23.
410. Deuteronomy 26:1–11.
411. Order of Seeds.
412. Order of Festivals.
413. I.e., tractates.
414. It occurs more often than any of the festivals. In fact, there are more Sabbaths during the year than the number of all the festivals combined.
415. Leviticus 23:1ff.
416. Leviticus 23:2.
417. Hebrew: fusions. Deals with laws pertaining to fusing abodes or domains on the Sabbath.
418. Hebrew: Pascal lambs. Deals with laws of Passover.
419. Exodus 12:1ff.
420. Leviticus 23: 5.
421. Plural of *Shekel*, an ancient Hebrew coin. Deals with laws pertaining to the payment of the *Shekel* tax for the Temple upkeep.

422. The Sabbath is mentioned in Exodus 16:23–30 and 20:8–11; Passover is mentioned in Exodus 21:1–28 and 23:15, whereas the law of the *Shekel* is not mentioned until Exodus 30:11–16.

423. Tractate Yoma. Lit.: the Day. Deals with laws of the Day of Atonement.

424. Exodus 30:11–16.

425. Leviticus 16:1–28.

426. Lit.: the matters of.

427. Pesachim.

428. Hebrew: *Sukkot,* or "booths."

429. Hebrew: *Shavuot,* or "weeks."

430. Lit.: egg. From the first word of this tractate. This tractate is also known as *Masekhet Yom Tov* meaning Festival Tractate, since it deals with laws of Festivals in general.

431. Lit.: booth or tabernacle.

432. Booths. Plural of *Sukkah.*

433. Lit.: head of the year. Deals with laws of the New Year.

434. Rebbe, compiler of the Mishnah.

435. Hebrew: *Tzomot.*

436. *Taanit,* singular of *Taniyot.*

437. Megillah, lit.: scroll. Deals with the laws of Purim and the Book of Esther.

438. About 200 years elapsed from the time of the destruction of the First Temple in 576 B.C.E. when fast days were decreed, until the decree of Purim during the reign of Artaxerxes the Second, 404–361 B.C.E.

439. Lit.: small or minor festival. Deals with laws of the intermediate days of Passover and tabernacles, i.e., semi-festive times.

440. Mo'ed Katan 13:9.

441. Lit.: topics or chapters.

442. Lit.: festal offering.

443. Exodus 23:17.

444. Order of Women.

445. Lit.: sisters-in-law. Deals with laws of Levirate marriage.

446. Lit.: marriage settlements.

447. I.e., optional.

448. Duty of a man to marry his deceased brother's childless widow.

449. The Courts.

450. The Levir.

451. The ceremony of removing the shoe and spitting if a man does not wish to contract Levirate marriage.

452. Such as Levirate marriage.

453. Rebbe, compiler of the Mishnah.

454. Lit.: vows.

455. Numbers 30:17.

456. Nezirut, lit.: the state of being under obligation of a Nazirite vow: this tractate is generally referred to as Nazir (lit.: one who is a Nazirite).

457. Chronologically: one must marry before one can get divorced.

458. Lit.: divorce.

459. Lit.: suspected adulteress.

460. Lit.: both of the pair.

461. Lit.: consecration. Deals with laws pertaining to betrothal and marriage.

462. To consummate regular and Levirate marriages.

463. I.e., follow one another.

464. Rebbe, compiler of the Mishnah.

465. Deuteronomy 24:1–2.

466. Kiddushin 5a.

467. I.e., betrothal.

468. I.e., divorce. Just as divorce is effected through a document, so too betrothal can be effected by a deed. Thus the scriptural sequence is divorce and then marriage. There are numerous other interpretations of this scriptural passage. See Gittin 90a, Ketubot 46b, Kiddushin 67b, etc.

469. Lit.: damages, the fourth Order of the Mishnah.

470. There may have been originally a single tractate entitled Nezikin (Damages) composed of what are today three separate tractates: Bava Kamma, Bava Metzia, and Bava Batra.

471. Lit.: first gate.

472. By fire or by eating; Exodus 22:4–5.

473. He must concern himself with removal of a public danger prior to judging guilt or innocence of a specific manifestation of that danger.

474. Lit.: middle gate.

475. I.e., property entrusted for keeping.

476. Exodus 21:38.

477. Ibid., 21:33.

478. Ibid., 22:4–5.

479. Ibid., 21:22.

480. An unpaid bailee, a paid trustee, a borrower, and a hired laborer. Exodus 22:6–14.

481. Lit.: last gate.

482. Securities or collateral.

483. Bava Batra, the third part of this large tractate.

484. Lit.: higher courts. Deals with the composition, powers, and functions of the courts.

485. Lit.: beatings. Deals with the laws of corporal punishment.

486. Old editions or copies.

487. If counted as a single tractate, Sanhedrin and Makkot would render the total tractate count in the Mishnah to sixty.

488. Rebbe, compiler of the Mishnah.

489. The title of the final chapter of Sanhedrin in the Mishnah, Maimonides' Commentary thereon, and the Jerusalem Talmud. However, in the Babylonian Talmud, Chapters 10 and 11 of tractate Sanhedrin are reversed.

490. The third chapter of Makkot.

491. Makkot.

492. Makkot 23a. The most prominent judge recites the scriptural verses, the second counts the strokes and the third says "strike."

493. Deuteronomy 25:2.

494. Lit.: oaths. Deals with laws pertaining to the various types of oaths.

495. Shevu'ot 3a.

496. Shevu'ot.

497. I.e., flogging.

498. Both of which only judges can do.

499. Rebbe, compiler of the Mishnah.

500. Eduyot; lit.: testimonies. It is a collection of miscellaneous traditions.

501. Lit.: to give you.

502. I.e., decisions.

503. Hebrew: *Halakhah LeMaaseh.*

504. *Bet Din.* This last sentence is very difficult in the Hebrew.

505. Deals with matters that arise nearly daily in an average life.

506. That which comes regularly takes precedence over that which comes infrequently. Berakhot 51b.

507. Avodah Zarah. Lit.: strange worship. Deals with rites and cults of idolators.

508. Hebrew: *Shabetai.* Shabbat 156a.

509. Hebrew: *Noga.*

510. Lit.: seeks out.

511. Hebrew: *Tzedek.*

512. Hebrew: *Maadim.* Shabbat 129b.

513. Sanhedrin 61a. One is only culpable through the normal mode of worship of an idol.

514. Avot. Lit.: fathers or principles. Contains aphorisms and maxims of ethics and morality.

515. Refers to Sages who have studied under the leading talmudic scholars of the previous generation, who in turn have studied among the leading talmudic scholars of the generation before that, etc., indicating the direct lineal descent from the original Sages who carried the tradition.

516. Rosh Hashanah 25a. The Mishnah continues: "Why were not the names of the Elders mentioned? To teach us that every group of three that acted as a court over Israel is equivalent to the Court of Moses."

517. Kafich's Hebrew edition erroneously has Samuel.

518. Ibid., 25b. The wording in the Gemara substitutes Bedan for Samson.

519. Deuteronomy 1:17.

520. Rebbe, compiler of the Mishnah.

521. Since other people will shy away from persons of ill repute.

522. Lit.: delay.

523. Avot 1:1.

524. Lit.: they of blessed memory.

525. Sanhedrin 32b. A case in which the judge feels or suspects the plaintiff or defendent or witness of being dishonest requires prolonged inquiry and investigation to ascertain the truth. The judge must feel that his judgment is in accordance with the feelings of his conscience, as to the truth or justice in this situation.

526. Avot 5:8.

527. The judge.

528. Lit.: lest the witnesses learn from his words.

529. Avot 1:9.

530. Ibid. Lit.: preparing the judges. See also Ketubot 86a.

531. Lit.: before the multitudes.

532. And then his judgment will not be accepted by the masses.

533. Since they have no one to turn to for justice and advice save this judge alone, and the latter's haughtiness and inaccessibility may drive the poor and oppressed to unethical or criminal practices.

534. Lit.: so that he not make light of peoples' merits. Idleness and luxuries of life may pervert a judge's mind away from the truth.

535. I.e., be not overconfident in rendering judgment without fear and trepidation. Avot 4:7.

536. Lit.: make a compromise.

537. Lit.: defend himself.

538. The judge.

539. The litigants.

540. I.e., no real evidence is being presented; only loquacious oratory.

541. Makkot 22b.

542. Ketubot 85a.

543. Firmnesses or resolutenesses, i.e., enforced judgments.

544. Sanhedrin 6b, i.e., take its course.

545. *Convolvulus scammonia.*

546. *Citrullus colocynthis schard.*

547. Lit.: abhorred or detested.

548. Lit.: if he cannot.

549. The judge.

550. Lit.: (unjust) profit. Exodus 18:21.

551. Proverbs 29:4.

552. I.e., is independent of other people and/or their favors.

553. I.e., he stabilizes it.

554. E.g., a judge who accepts bribes "overthrows" the land. See Ketubot 105b and Sanhedrin 7b.

555. Makkot, Shevu'ot, etc. accompany Sanhedrin in that all deal with judges and their functions.

556. Avot.

557. Alternate translation: learning or wisdom.

558. I.e., fear of God.

559. Rebbe, compiler of the Mishnah.

560. Lit.: rulings. Deals with erroneous rulings of religious courts.

561. Seder Kodashim.

562. Some texts substitute "sacrifices of the priests."

563. Lit.: slaughterings or sacrifices.

564. Lit.: meal offerings. Deals with meal and drink offerings.

565. The former is in the first chapter of Leviticus, the latter in the second chapter.

566. Deuteronomy 12:14.

567. Ibid., 12:15.

568. Lit.: Nonholy. Deals with laws of slaughtering for ordinary consumption. Also contains the dietary laws.

569. Lit.: firstborn. Deals with laws of firstborn humans or animals.

570. Deuteronomy 12:17.

571. I.e., sacrifices and firstborns.

572. Arakhin. Lit.: estimations. Deals with laws pertaining to the redemption of holy objects.

573. Lit.: substitution. Deals with laws pertaining to substitution of one offering for another.

574. Arakhin is discussed in Leviticus 27:1–8, whereas Temurah is mentioned in Leviticus 27:9–10.

575. Lit.: extirpations.

576. Usually interpreted as Heavenly punishment or "cutting off" from one's people as Scriptures state: *That soul shall be utterly cut off, his iniquity shall be upon him* (Numbers 15:31).

577. Such as the Pascal offering (Numbers 9:13) and Circumcision (Genesis 17:14), willful transgression of which incur the *Karet* penalty; but unintentional omission does not require a sin offering.

578. Keritot 1:1.

579. Lit.: trespass. Deals with the laws of sacrilege or misappropriation of sanctuary property. Leviticus 5:14–16.

580. A sin offering is brought for an unintentional transgression that if willfully done, would have incurred the death penalty. A trespass offering, however, is brought for an unintentional transgression that if willfully committed, would incur only the flogging penalty.

581. Lit.: regular, always. Deals with "regular" or daily sacrifices.

582. Derived through one of the thirteen principles of rabbinic exegesis.

583. I.e., when the Temple will be rebuilt.

584. Lit.: measures

585. I.e., length, width, height, and other measurements.

586. God, perhaps referring to a prophet. Some texts have "holy spirit."

587. 1 Chronicles 28:19.

588. Lit.: nests. Deals with laws of bird offerings. These are usually offered in pairs, two doves, two pigeons, etc.; one a sin offering and the other a burnt offering. Hence, plural *Kinnim* is used.

589. In tractate Kinnim.

590. Lit.: occupied himself with the subdivision of.

591. Lit.: purifications. This order is not called by its antonym "Uncleanlinesses" or "Defilements" (Hebrew: *Tumot*) because most of the tractates therein deal with ways and means for ritual purification. Another reason for not using the antonym is that talmudic and biblical writings use euphemisms in order to avoid disrespectful language.

592. Lit.: vessels.

593. Hebrew: *Avot HaTumot*. Lit.: the fathers of defilements.

594. Lit.: tents.

595. Through overshadowing by a tent in which the corpse is contained. Numbers 19:14–16.

596. A corpse is considered the "father of fathers" of defilement.

597. Lit.: plagues or leprosies.

598. Just as with a corpse, all that is also present in the tent becomes defiled by overshadowing. However, the resemblance is not complete. A corpse defiles other objects to the primary degree of defilement (father of defilement) and these, in turn, can defile man and vessels, whereas a leper defiles other objects to a secondary degree, so that these, in turn, can only defile food and beverages.

599. Defilement of and by a leper.

600. One defiled by a corpse is purified by sprinkling water mixed with ashes of the red heifer on the third and seventh days after defilement. Numbers 19:19.

601. Lit.: heifer or cow.

602. I.e., "fathers" of defilement.

603. Such people can become purified on the same day as their defilement occurred, but only after sunset and ritual immersion.

604. Lit.: purification.

605. As opposed to calling it tractate Tumot, defilements. See also footnote 591.

606. Some texts add the words "purification from."

607. Lit.: incorrect.

608. See *Maimonides' Treatise on Logic* by I. Efros (New York, American Academy for Jewish Research, 1938), chap. 13, p. 60, where Maimonides states: "A term used in general and in particular is one that designates any species

by the name of its genus, e.g., the word *Kokhav* applied to any star of heaven, though it is the name of one of the seven planets (Mercury) and the word *hashish* in Arabic given to all kinds of grass and to the yellow flower used in dyeing."

609. Lit.: ritual immersion pools.

610. Lit.: menstruant.

611. Only women.

612. Lit.: sufferers of flux.

613. Lit.: predispositions. Deals with conditions, mainly wetting of foods by liquids, which predispose to defilement. Leviticus 11:34.

614. Leviticus 9:1.

615. Ibid. 14:2.

616. Hebrew: Immersed at daytime or for one day. Deals with laws pertaining to a man unclean until sundown.

617. Leviticus 15:32.

618. Hebrew: Hands. Deals with laws of ritual uncleanness due to unwashed hands.

619. Lit.: stems. Deals with laws pertaining to defilements of stalks, skins, seeds, and stems of fruits.

620. Rebbe completed the Mishnah.

621. Originally the number of tractates was sixty because Makkot was combined with Sanhedrin into a single tractate (Midrash Rabbah on Song of Songs 6:9). If Bava Kamma, Bava Metzia, and Bava Batra are counted as three separate tractates, this would make a total of sixty-three. The very small tractates such as Sofrim (Scribes), Semahot (Rejoicings), Kallah (Bride), Derekh Eretz (Way of the Land or Etiquette, actually two tractates), Gerim (Strangers or Converts to Judaism), Kutim (Cuthites), Tzitzit (Fringes), are

not included in the count. These were later incorporated into the Babylonian Talmud.

622. Our Mishnah texts have a fourth chapter in tractate Bikkurim entitled *Androgenes* (Hermaphrodite) which is not found in Maimonides' Commentary. This would raise the total number of chapters in the six orders of the Mishnah to 524.

623. Rebbe.

624. Only Simeon the Righteous, last of the Sages of the Great Assembly, and those who succeeded him are mentioned, since Simeon was chronologically the closest to Rebbe of all the Sages of the Great Assembly.

625. See note 623.

626. Lit.: many topics. Probably refers to tractate Avot.

627. Lit.: hard on him.

628. Stenographic brevity suffices for themselves.

629. See note 623.

630. Independent Mishnah compilation in the form of a supplement.

631. Rabbi Hiyah.

632. The redaction of the *Tosefta* is attributed to both Rabbi Hiyah and Rabbi Oshayah.

633. Extraneous Mishnah. Includes all Tannaitic statements excluded from the Mishnah.

634. *Torat Kohanim*, a halakhic commentary on Leviticus.

635. A halakhic commentary on Numbers and Deuteronomy.

636. For example: Sukkah 54a.

637. Lit.: not like the order of its topics.

638. Song of Songs 6:9. These derivative words, "daughters" of the Mishnah, reveal its merits in comparison

with the *Tosefta, Beraita, Sifra, Sifre,* etc. The praise that Solomon heaps upon his beloved is allegorically compared to the praise heaped upon the Mishnah.

639. Rebbe, compiler of the Mishnah.

640. Rabbis Hiyah, Oshayah, and Rav.

641. I.e., as time passes, explanations of the Mishnah text are forgotten or misinterpreted or somewhat altered.

642. Lit.: the true argument.

643. Lit.: the main goal of his goals.

644. Lit.: relied upon.

645. Lit.: established.

646. Rav Ashi.

647. Lit.: against common sense.

648. I.e., make these matters abstruse or subtle.

649. Kiddushin 71a.

650. Lit.: secrets.

651. Hagigah 13a.

652. Refers to the esoteric aspects of creation and does not include the whole talmudic cosmogony, as discussed in the second chapter of tractate Hagigah.

653. Ezekiel's prophetic career (Ezekiel, Chap. 1) is introduced by the vision of the Divine Chariot. Although Isaiah also had a similar vision (Isaiah, chap. 6), no wheels were seen by Isaiah, whereas Ezekiel's chariot was mobile. Maimonides, in the introduction to his *Guide for the Perplexed,* states that the "Work of the Chariot" refers to metaphysics, whereas the "Work of the Creation" denotes material science. A complete exposition of the "Work of the Chariot" and comparisons of the visions of Ezekiel and Isaiah is provided by Maimonides in his *Guide for the Perplexed* (Part III,

NOTES

Chaps. 5–7). See also Maimonides' *Mishneh Torah, Laws Concerning the Basic Principles of the Torah* chap. 4:10–11.
654. Lit.: in their hand.
655. Song of Songs 4:11.
656. The Talmud (Hagigah 13a) continues: "The things that are sweeter than honey and milk should be under thy tongue," i.e., the mysteries of the Chariot may not be taught.
657. Some versions substitute the word *learn* for the word *teach*.
658. Lit.: made himself fit.
659. I.e., the hidden allusions.
660. Psalms 119:18.
661. Because it is beyond the fool's comprehension.
662. Proverbs 23:9.
663. Ibid. 1:6.
664. Different body temperaments and constitutions are described in detail in several of Maimonides' medical writings, especially his *Medical Aphorisms*. In brief, health is dependent on homeostasis of the four body humors: blood, white bile (phlegm), black bile (melancholy), and yellow bile. Derangement of normal equilibrium of these humors leads to illness. This was the ancient and medieval concept of health and disease.
665. The sun.
666. This is the Ptolemaic theory. The Maimonidean mile may not be identical with the talmudic mile, which in turn is less than the Roman mile.
667. Medicine, arithmetic, music, and the natural sciences.

668. Lit.: cannot be reached.

669. Lit.: null and void.

670. Astronomy.

671. A famous book on astronomy written by the philosopher Ptolemy and twice translated into Arabic. Maimonides probably did not read Greek and therefore must have utilized an Arabic translation.

672. Stated by Ptolemy above.

673. Just as he accepts the existence of the sun, so too will he believe in the quoted measurements thereof.

674. Other than astronomy.

675. The Arabic term includes mathematics, geometry, astronomy, and music. These sciences sharpen the mind of man and help him understand divine matters.

676. See *Maimonides' Treatise on Logic* by I. Efros (New York: American Academy for Jewish Research, 1938) where, in Chapter 14, Maimonides states as follows: "Theoretical philosophy is divided into three parts: mathematics, physics, and theology. Mathematics studies material things not as they are but as abstracted from, though always existing in matter. The parts of this science which are its roots are four: arithmetic, geometry, astronomy, and music; and these parts constitute what is called the propaedeutic science. Physics studies material things existing, not as products of human will but in nature, e.g., minerals, plants, and animals. . . . Theology is divided into two parts. One of them is the study of every being which is not matter nor a force in matter, that is to say, of whatever appertains to God. . . . The other part of theology studies the remote causes of the subject matter of the other sciences, and is called both Divine science and metaphysics. . . ."

677. Is not knowledgeable in any science.

678. He failed to study during his youth and prior to marriage, which is the best learning period.

679. Lit.: accustom ourselves.

680. Lit.: they, of blessed memory.

681. Lit.: all that is in the world.

682. Eruvin 53a.

683. Intellectual powers.

684. A chamber in the Holy Temple whose door measured twenty cubits in width.

685. Some texts omit the words "not even." The meaning is unchanged.

686. Isaiah 29:14.

687. See Ezekiel 14:21.

688. The Sages of old.

689. Gittin 57a.

690. Lit.: the entire night. See also Maimonides' *Mishneh Torah, Laws Dealing with the Study of Torah* 3:13, where he states: "While it is a duty by day and by night, most of one's knowledge is acquired at night. Therefore, he who desires to merit the crown of the Torah should be heedful of all his nights and not waste even a single one of them in sleep, eating, drinking, idle talk, and so forth. Rather, [he should devote all of them] to the study of Torah and words of wisdom. The Sages have stated that the reservoir of Torah is the night as it is written (Lamentations 2:19): *Arise, cry out in the night,* and whosoever occupies himself with [the study of] Torah at night—a mark of grace distinguishes him by day as it is written (Psalms 42:9): *By day the Lord will command His loving-kindness and in the night His song shall be with me, even a prayer unto the God of my life.*"

691. Study Torah early in the day and late in the day, for during the main portion of the day a person is occupied with his livelihood.

692. The learning of Torah.

693. Berakhot 8a.

694. Although Shem and his descendant Eber were believed to have maintained schools (see Rashi's commentary on Genesis 25:22 and Genesis Rabbah 63:6), these schools preceded the giving of the Torah by God on Mount Sinai, and thus *halakhah* could not have been taught in the sense that we know it today.

695. Probably ancient philosophers and not Sages.

696. See also Maimonides' *Guide for the Perplexed*, Part 3, Chapter 25, where he states: "The philosophers [probably referring to Aristotle] assume that in Nature there is nothing in vain, so that everything that is not the product of human industry serves a certain purpose. . . ." Also see Maimonides' *Treatise on Logic*, Chapter 9, where he states: "The causes of things are of four kinds: matter, form, agent, and purpose. Let us take, for example, among artificial things, a chair; its matter is the wood, its agent is the carpenter, its form is a square if it is square . . . and its purpose is the sitting thereon . . . In the case of natural things one should seek the very same causes; for example, man belongs to the natural order, his matter is life, his form is the rational faculty, his purpose is the attainment of ideas, and his agent is the one who gave him his form or his rational faculty . . . and this is God, Blessed be He. . . ."

697. 1 Kings 3:12: *Behold I have given thee a wise and understanding* heart . . ., and 1 Kings 5:26: *And the Lord gave Solomon wisdom.*

698. Ibid., 5:13.

699. Ibid., 5:14.

700. *Aconitum Pesicum Eisenhut.*

701. An herb with red sap; perhaps *Calamus Dracol, Dracaena Cinnabari Balp.*

702. See Shabbat 77b. "Rav Judah said in Rav's name: Of all that the Holy One, Blessed be He, created in His world, He did not create a single thing without purpose. Thus He created the snail as a remedy for a scab, the fly as an antidote to the hornet's sting, the mosquito for a serpent's bite, a serpent as a remedy for an eruption, and a spider as a remedy for a scorpion's bite. . . ."

703. Which is a small bird that makes its nest within houses during the warm season.

704. Some texts have: such as the lion that preys.

705. See also Maimonides' *Guide for the Perplexed*, Part 1, Chapter 68, where he discusses the subject of *intellectus*, the *ens intelligens* and the *ens intelligibile.*

706. Some texts omit: or to be a king.

707. Some Hebrew texts have the word *Penimi* meaning "internal." The Hebrew word *Penimi* as found in Proverbs 3:15 means "ruby" or "coral" or "precious stone."

708. I.e., eating, drinking, etc.

709. See Maimonides' *Mishneh Torah, Laws of the Fundamental Principles of the Torah* 4:8, where he states: "The superior intelligence found in the human soul is the form of man complete with knowledge. To this form, the Torah refers in the text: *Let us make man in our image, after our likeness* (Genesis 1:26). This means that man should have a form which understands and grasps knowledges that have no form. . . ."

710. That God is eternal, incorporeal, etc. See Maimonides' *Mishneh Torah, Laws of the Fundamental Principles of the Torah*, Chapter 1. See also Maimonides' *Mishnah Commentary on Tractate Sanhedrin*, Chapter 10, where he enunciates and expounds upon the thirteen articles or principles of the Jewish faith.

711. Bodies of knowledge.

712. Many disparaging references are found to ostriches in Jewish sources.

713. See Genesis 1:2. *And the earth was wasteness and emptiness.*

714. Wise in intellect and good in morals and ethics.

715. Some texts have wisdom.

716. Proper eating and drinking habits, etc.

717. Ethical attributes such as honesty, kindness, etc.

718. Aristotle.

719. Discerning in wisdom and righteous in deeds.

720. See also Maimonides' "Eight Chapters" or Introduction to his Commentary on Tractate Avot, where in Chapter 5, he states, "Man must keep his eye constantly fixed upon one goal, namely the attainment of the knowledge of God, may He be blessed, as far as it is possible . . . man's only purpose in eating, drinking, cohabiting, sleeping, waking, moving about and resting should be the preservation of bodily health, while, in turn, the reason for the latter is that the soul and its agencies may be in sound and perfect condition so that he may readily acquire wisdom, and gain moral and intellectual virtues. . . ."

721. Jeremiah 8:8.

722. Jeremiah continues: *Lo, they have rejected the word of the Lord, and what wisdom is in them?*

723. Lit.: intermediate.

724. Who is wise and discerning but who lusts for worldly pleasures.

725. His deeds are not performed because of a clear understanding and basic comprehension of his purpose in life.

726. Avot 2:5.

727. In that piety is incomplete without wisdom, understanding, and knowledge.

728. Deuteronomy 5:1.

729. Kiddushin 40b.

730. Lit.: conceptionalization or rationality, i.e., wisdom.

731. Who lived 969 years. Genesis 5:26–27.

732. He finds all his needs taken care of by others.

733. The ancient Greeks divided the earth into seven regions or seven different climates; the first and seventh are uninhabitable. Therefore, Maimonides states from the second to the sixth.

734. Lit.: three spirits. In the first chapter of his "Eight Chapters," Maimonides speaks of five parts to the human soul: the nutritive, the perceptive, the imaginative, the appetitive, and the rational.

735. Lit.: people of the land or of the earth.

736. The Sages.

737. The unlearned people.

738. Some texts have: possessions.

739. See Maimonides' *Treatise on Poisons*, ed. S. Muntner (Philadelphia, J. B. Lippincott, 1966).

740. Isaiah 25:1.

741. Berakhot 58a.

742. The Talmud continues: "For Ben Zoma used to say: What labors Adam had to carry out before he obtained bread to eat! He plowed, he sowed, he reaped, he bound, he threshed and winnowed and selected the ears; he ground and sifted, he kneaded and baked and then at last he ate; whereas I get up and find all these things done for me. And how many labors Adam had to carry out before he obtained a garment to wear! He had to shear, wash [the wool], comb it, spin it, weave it. . . ."

743. The Moon, Mercury, Venus, Sun, Mars, Jupiter, Saturn, and the East to West spheres. See Maimonides' *Mishneh Torah, Laws of the Fundamental Principles of the Torah,* Chapter 3.

744. Fire, air, water, earth. Ibid., Chapter 4.

745. Those destined to go to Heaven. Lit.: those who will ascend.

746. Sukkah 45b.

747. More important than the first reason for the creation of the masses, namely to provide sustenance for the wise.

748. Exodus 23:29.

749. Ecclesiastes 12:13.

750. Berakhot 6b.

751. See Maimonides' *Mishneh Torah, Laws of the Fundamental Principles of the Torah* 4:3-4.

752. Berakhot 8a. *Halakhah* refers not only to practical deeds but also to spiritual matters.

753. Daniel 4:5.

754. The Talmud itself, in Bava Metzia 86a, ascribes its redaction to both Rav Ashi (375-427) and Ravina, son of Rav Huna (474-499). Rav Ashi compiled the first draft but

its completion was only accomplished seventy years later by Ravina, after the death of Rav Ashi.

755. Mishnah Order of Seeds.

756. Mishnah Order of Festivals.

757. Mishnah Order of Damages.

758. Mishnah Order of Holy Things.

759. Mishnah Order of Purifications.

760. Also called the Palestinian Talmud–approximately 100 years before the Babylonian Talmud.

761. Independent supplementary Mishnah compilation.

762. Extraneous Mishnah, which includes all Tannaitic statements excluded from the Mishnah.

763. Maimonides' Mishnah Commentary on Seder Tohorot.

764. The Talmud, in Bava Metzia 86a, in describing authorship of the Talmud places Rav Ashi before Ravina. Here and in other places both in the Talmud and in Maimonides' writings, where Ravina's name precedes Rav Ashi, it probably refers not to Ravina the redactor of the Talmud but to another Ravina.

765. The Talmud is not to be added to or deleted from.

766. *Geonim* are heads of the Babylonian academies who followed the *Tanna'im* and *Amora'im*, Sages of the Mishnah and Gemara respectively.

767. Codes without the preliminary lengthy discussions leading to such judgments as found in the Talmud.

768. Or *Great Halakhot* composed by Rabbi Simon Kairo in the year 4501 of the Hebrew calendar corresponding to 741 C.E.

769. Attributed to the Gaon Rabbi Judah. Some texts substitute *Halakhot Ketanot*.

770. Composed by Gaon Rabbi Jehudai, a blind scholar who succeeded to the *Gaonate* of Sura in 760 C.E.

771. More popularly known as the *She'eltot* (Discussions) oɪ Rav Aha.

772. Isaac, the son of Jacob Alfasi (1013–1103), born near Fez, Morocco, but migrated to Spain. His compendium of the Talmud eliminated all irrelevant discussions and formulated clear-cut decisions on Jewish legal matters.

773. Laws applicable outside the Holy Land.

774. Lit.: do not reach ten under any circumstance.

775. Maimonides is now speaking of himself and his own generation.

776. To devote ourselves to Torah study and practice.

777. Rabbi Maimon.

778. Joseph the son of Meir Ibn Megash HaLevi 1077–1141, who at the age of 26 succeeded Alfasi at the latter's request in the rabbinate at Lucena, Spain. Rabbi Joseph Ibn Megash was the teacher of Rabbi Maimon, father of Moses Maimonides.

779. Lit.: may God live.

780. 2 Kings 23:25.

781. This probably refers to the writings of Rabbi Joseph Ibn Megash in addition to the writings of Rabbi Maimon, which comment on the words of Ibn Megash.

782. Hullin deals with dietary laws, laws of slaughtering, etc.

783. The Mishnah would be unintelligible without the Gemara to explain it.

784. Maimonides, in his *Commentary on the Mishnah*, introduces a subject, then describes general principles thereof, then goes into the details and then provides the final deci-

sion. This is the methodology of studying Talmud that he advocates.

785. Probably an allusion to Exodus 18:9: *and for a memorial between thine eyes, that the law of the Lord may be in thy mouth;* it will be fixed in his mind's eye and organized for ready quotation.

786. The commentary on the Mishnah.

787. I.e., those with "hearts of stone."

788. The Mishnah, in the first chapter of tractate Eduyot, enumerates the cases in which the final decision is in accord with the school of Shammai, as well as the instances where the final decision follows neither the view of the schools of Hillel or Shammai.

789. The Talmud itself in Shabbat 46a states "The *Halakhah* [legal decision] is [always] as an anonymous mishnah," that is, if a mishnah bears no name, it represents the final decision of Rebbe, the redactor of the Mishnah and his colleagues.

790. Such as an anonymous mishnah followed by a dispute, e.g., Yevamot 42b.

791. Lit.: to think about them.

792. See Exodus 23:2: *the verdict should always be according to the majority.* Although the majority rule is generally accepted, this rule will nevertheless be cited wherever it is applied.

793. Falseness.

794. I.e., the Mishnah commentary.

795. Lit.: deals with the number of Sages.

796. Such as Rabbi Simeon without specifying which Rabbi Simeon.

797. Lit.: add to their clarification.

798. Some texts substitute Hananiah.

799. An additional name, Aba Elazar ben Dolai, is inserted here in the edition of Dr. Hamburgher. This name is lacking in all the Hebrew and Arabic manuscripts, however.

800. Some texts read Hananiah.

801. See note 800.

802. Some texts have Elhanan.

803. This name is present in the original Arabic manuscript but lacking in the Hebrew texts.

804. Some texts have Jose.

805. Some texts combine 86 and 87 into Rabbi Yadua the Babylonian. Kafich points out that Yadua did not have the title Rabbi and hence 86 and 87 are separate.

806. There are additional Sages in the Mishnah that Maimonides does not enumerate here. Perhaps his Mishnah texts in manuscript form were different from those we know today. The Sages of the Mishnah are listed chronologically in Danby's *The Mishnah* (Oxford University Press, 1958), p. 799.

807. One of the first post-Tannaitic Sages. He is mentioned in Avot 6:2 and Uktzin 3:12.

808. Lit.: Samuel the small.

809. Ninety-one in the first section above and the thirty-seven just enumerated.

810. Avot 4:20; also known as Elisha ben Abuyah who was guilty of apostasy and heresy. See Hagigah 15a.

811. Hagigah 2:2.

812. Menahem was also said to be guilty of apostasy. See Hagigah 16b.

813. Some texts erroneously omit the words "son of

Rabban Simeon." Evidence for the correctness of including these words comes from Maimonides' Introduction to his *Mishneh Torah*.

814. See the Jerusalem Talmud, Kilayim, Chapter 9.

815. See Yoma 71b and Gittin 57b.

816. Deuteronomy 33:10.

817. Mentioned in Zevahim 1:2.

818. Parah 3:5.

819. Ibid.

820. Ibid.

821. Ibid.

822. As opposed to Priests or Levites.

823. 586 B.C.E. to 79 C.E.

824. Some texts add here Rabbi Elazar of Modi'im who was already enumerated in the previous generation.

825. Grandson of Rabbi Ishmael ben Elisha the High Priest mentioned above.

826. At the beginning of Maimonides' Introduction to Seder Zera'im.

827. Possibly referring to the legend in the Talmud, Bava Metzia 59b, in which Rabbi Eliezer maintained his view against the majority in declaring the oven of Aknai not liable to ritual uncleanness. For his insistence, Rabbi Eliezer was excommunicated. Alternately, Maimonides may be referring to another story concerning Rabbi Eliezer ben Hyrcanus related in Midrash Rabbah on Genesis (beginning of Chapter 42) and in the Mishnah Avot of Rabbi Nathan (Chapter 6). See also Pirké de Rabbi Eliezer, Chapters 1 and 2.

828. Hagigah 14b.

829. Lit.: my teacher.

830. Ketubot 84b has a discussion as to whether Rabbi Akiba was Rabbi Tarfon's colleague or pupil.

831. *Sifra* Leviticus, Chapter 4, Section 37, commenting on the fifth verse of the first chapter of Leviticus.

832. Eruvin 13a where it states, "Rabbi Meir related: When I was with Rabbi Ishmael I used to put vitriol into my ink [for writing sacred scrolls and texts] and he told me nothing [against it], but when I subsequently came to Rabbi Akiba, the latter forbade it to me. . . ."

833. Yevamot 84a where it states, "Rebbe related: When I went to learn Torah at the school of Rabbi Elazar ben Shamua, his disciples combined against me like the cocks of Bet Bukya and did not let me learn more than this single thing in our Mishnah. . . ."

834. See Nazir 49b and Kiddushin 52b where it states, "Our Rabbis taught: After the demise of Rabbi Meir, Rabbi Judah announced to his pupils: Let not Rabbi Meir's disciples enter hither, because they are argumentative and do not come to learn the Torah. . . ."

835. Such as Rabbi Simeon without specifying which Rabbi Simeon.

836. Temurah 15b and Bava Kamma 103b. The Talmud continues, "He was either Rabbi Judah ben Baba or Rabbi Judah ben Ilai. . . ."

837. Rabbi Elazar's.

838. Rabbi Judah the Prince or Rebbe.

839. See footnote 814, above.

840. One story is related in the Talmud, Shabbat 33b, where Rabbi Simeon ben Yohai and his son Elazar lived and studied in a cave for thirteen years, after fleeing from the

Roman authorities for uttering anti-Gentile statements. Another story, in Me'ilah 17b, relates the miraculous cure of the Emperor's daughter by Rabbi Simeon ben Yohai who was rewarded by having the oppressive decree against the Jews annulled.

841. The prayer entitled *Al HaNissim*, which is uttered daily during the eight-day holiday of *Hanukkah*.

842. Horayot 13b: "Rabbi Simeon ben Gamliel was the President [of the Sanhedrin or *Nasi*]; Rabbi Meir was the Sage [*Hakham*] and Rabbi Nathan the Vice-President [*Ab-bet-din*]. Whenever Rabbi Simeon ben Gamliel entered, all the people stood up for him; when Rabbi Meir and Rabbi Nathan entered, all the people stood up for them also." Rabbi Simeon, in order to distinguish his office from those of Rabbi Meir and Rabbi Nathan issued a decree that the people not rise for Rabbi Meir and Rabbi Nathan. As a result, when the people did not rise for Rabbi Meir and Rabbi Nathan on the following day, the latter attempted to retaliate by requesting Rabbi Simeon to expound upon the tractate of Uktzin, with which the latter was not familiar. The plot was discovered and Rabbi Meir and Rabbi Nathan were expelled from the rabbinical College of Rabbi Simeon.

843. Horayot 13b–14a.

844. Eruvin 13a.

845. Sanhedrin 17b.

846. Rashi and others state that the third Simeon mentioned anonymously in the Gemara refers to Rabbi Simeon the Temanite.

847. The Talmud Sanhedrin 17b has Hananiah ben Hakinai.

848. *Nehora* in Aramaic is Meir in Hebrew.

849. Eruvin 13b. In his Introduction to the *Mishneh Torah*, Maimonides declares that Rabbi Nehemiah was Rabbi Meir's friend. Perhaps there were two Rabbis Nehemiah.

850. To express one person's name by the plural word *Sages*.

851. Lit.: house

852. See note 851.

853. See Jerusalem Talmud, Shabbat 1:3 and 10:4.

854. Eruvin 96b.

855. Lit.: clarifies them.

856. You will know when the final decision is not in accordance with an anonymous Mishnah, and which anonymous Mishnah does not represent the view of Rabbi Meir.

857. Without the title Rabbi.

858. Isaiah and Jeremiah, not Rabbi Isaiah or Rabbi Jeremiah.

859. Actually only the Patriarchs from the House of Hillel were designated with the appellation Rabban.

860. See *Tosefta* on Eduyot 3:4, where it states, "Greater than a Rav is a Rabbi, greater than a Rabbi is a Rabban, and greater than Rabban is the name alone." See also the discussion in Sanhedrin 13b when it states that those who were ordained in the Holy Land were given the appellation Rabbi.

861. Equivalent to Rabbi Saul.

862. Zevahim 1:2.

863. It does not indicate a greater or lesser level of esteem.

864. Temurah 15b.

865. Lit.: except in rare occurrences.

866. Yevamot 49b.

867. The more statements found in the Mishnah by a particular Sage, the more likely there is to be found a dissenting viewpoint.

868. However, they may be mentioned again in ethical or homiletical connections.

869. Chapter 2:6.

870. Chapter 4:8 and Chapter 3:3, respectively. Kafich, quoting others, states that Hananiah ben Hakinai is mentioned in two other places in the Mishnah, Makkot 3:10, and Avot 3:4. These are not considered here by Maimonides because no legal ruling or other teaching can be derived therefrom.

871. Chapter 3:5 and Chapter 4:7, respectively. See also Bava Batra 92b, Nega'im 7:2 and 16:3, and Mikva'ot 8:3.

872. Chapter 10:6.

873. Chapter 1:4 and Chapter 2:5, respectively. See also Oholot 3:5, Zavim 3:1, and Tevul Yom 3:5.

874. Chapter 2:1. See also Nazir 32b and Bava Batra 78a.

875. Chapter 2:6 and Chapter 5:4, respectively.

876. Chapter 8:5 and Chapter 1:4, respectively.

877. Chapter 2:2.

878. Chapter 4:13 and Chapter 16:7, respectively. See also Taanit, Chapter 3, Betzah, Chapter 3, and Yadayim 1:3.

879. Chapter 5:3 and 5:5, respectively.

880. Chapter 7:9. See also Maaser Sheni 3:6, Makkot, Chapter 3, and Nega'im 10:8.

881. Chapter 1:5.

882. Chapter 8:1, Chapter 6:2, Chapter 8:2, Chapter 7:5, and Chapter 7:8, respectively.

883. Father of R. Elazar ben Azariah.

884. Chapter 1:2. See also Tohorot 8:7.

885. Chapter 4:4. See also Nega'im 12:3.

886. Chapter 4:6 is the reference quoted in some texts. However, our version of the Mishnah does not have a Rabbi Jacob in the aforementioned Mishnah. Perhaps Maimonides is referring to the Rabbi Jacob in Avot 4:16.

887. Chapter 2:10. This Sage is omitted in some texts.

888. Chapter 7:9.

889. Chapter 3:5.

890. This statement is not entirely true, as some of the Sages are mentioned more than once in the Mishnah. For example, Rabbi Elazar Hisma, number 5 in Maimonides' list, is also mentioned in Nega'im 7:2 and Mikva'ot 8:3. Similarly, Rabbi Simeon of Timna, number 21 in Maimonides' list, is also mentioned in Yadayim 1:3 and Taanit 3:7. This problem is discussed at length by Rabbi Reuben Margolies in Volume 10 of the Hebrew periodical *Sinai* in an essay entitled, *Regarding Maimonides' Introduction to the Mishnah*.

Dr. Fred Rosner

Fred Rosner, M.D., F.A.C.P., is director of the Department of Medicine of the Mount Sinai Services at the Queens Hospital Center and professor of medicine at New York's Mount Sinai School of Medicine. He is a diplomate of the American Board of Internal Medicine, a fellow of the American College of Physicians, and the recipient of numerous awards.

Dr. Rosner is an internationally known authority on medical ethics. He has lectured widely on Jewish medical ethics and is in great demand as a speaker on this and related topics. He has served as a visiting professor or lecturer in England, France, Germany, Mexico, Canada, Holland, Israel, South Africa, and throughout the United States. He is a member of the Professional Advisory Board of the prestigious Kennedy Institute for Ethics of Georgetown University, as well as chairman of the Medical Ethics Committee of the Medical Society of the State of New York.

He is the author of five widely acclaimed books on Jewish medical ethics, including *Modern Medicine and Jewish Ethics* and the two-volume *Medicine and Jewish Law*. These books are up-to-date examinations of the Jewish view on many important bioethical issues in medical practice. A noted Maimonidean scholar, Dr. Rosner has translated and published, in English, most of Maimonides' medical writings.

WITHDRAWN